838 WAYS TO AMUSE A CHILD

BOOKS BY JUNE JOHNSON

838 WAYS TO AMUSE A CHILD

HOME PLAY FOR THE PRESCHOOL CHILD

838

WAYS TO AMUSE A CHILD

CRAFTS, HOBBIES AND CREATIVE IDEAS
FOR THE CHILD FROM SIX TO TWELVE

REVISED EDITION

BY JUNE JOHNSON
DRAWINGS BY BERYL BENNETT

 HARPER COLOPHON BOOKS
Harper & Row, Publishers
New York, Cambridge, Philadelphia, San Francisco
London, Mexico City, São Paulo, Sydney

838 WAYS TO AMUSE A CHILD *(Revised Edition)*. Copyright © 1983 by June Johnson. All rights reserved. Printed in the United States of America. No part of this book may be used or reproduced in any manner whatsoever without written permission except in the case of brief quotations embodied in critical articles and reviews. For information address Harper & Row, Publishers, Inc., 10 East 53rd Street, New York, N.Y. 10022. Published simultaneously in Canada by Fitzhenry & Whiteside Limited, Toronto.

First HARPER COLOPHON edition published 1983.

Library of Congress Cataloging in Publication Data

Johnson, June.
    838 ways to amuse a child.

    (Harper colophon books; CN/1047)
    Includes bibliographical references and index.
    1. Indoor games. 2. Amusements. 3. Creative activities and seat work. I. Title. II
Title: Eight hundred thirty-eight ways to amuse a child.
GV1203.J65   1983   790.1′922   82-48801
ISBN 0-06-091047-X (pbk.)

---

83 84 85 86 87 10 9 8 7 6 5 4 3 2 1

To Phil
for 838 reasons

CONTENTS

INTRODUCTION

MUST I AMUSE MY CHILD?

You picked up this book because the title attracted you. *Hundreds* of ways to amuse a child. Imagine! Convalescence and travel, nature and science, crafts and hobbies—a long list, and how wonderful for Bob and Mary.

Now, perhaps, as you stand with the book in your hand, second, more serious thoughts assail you. "Have I the obligation to amuse my children?" you wonder. "Have I, really, even the right? If they don't learn to amuse themselves, to live their own lives, in these years from six to twelve—when do they?"

You are quite right. You do not have the obligation to provide amusement for your children—not most of the time, as a matter of policy. And your children do indeed have the right, the wonderfully important right, to amuse themselves. This book seeks only to spread before them the vast panorama of a child's world, for their own choice, at their own time, in their own individual way.

A NOTE ON THE BOOK

838 Ways to Amuse a Child has been written primarily for simple home play. In most cases, the suggestions do not depend on elaborate materials or tools or parental skills. An effort was made to avoid the type of book where the parent says as he reads, "This would be wonderful *if* I had the time . . . *or* we owned those tools . . . *or* I knew how

1

to . . . (read music, handle a jig saw, interpret scientific jargon)."

Young people, however, do need the tools of youth. They need balls and games and toys of all varieties. They need the supplies that make creative activities possible (these supplies are listed on p. 6). And certainly they need the books and records that mean so much to the growth of the inner youth. Fortunate the young people who grow up in a family that has the happy custom of giving books and records at each holiday.

This book lists a number of specific references after almost every subject covered. So many excellent juvenile books are published today, however, that no list could be complete. Therefore a number of more general references are given below.

GENERAL REFERENCES

American children are still watching TV—and now playing expensive video games—many hours a day. Such activities severely limit the wholesome outdoor exercise that leads to good health, positive attitudes, and comfortable social adjustment toward themselves, their peers, and their society.

Of equal importance, however, such let-the-world-entertain-me time-consuming activities cripple the youth's capacity for eager search and the excitement that results from exploring the world. The stretching young mind needs wholesome and filling food, just as the body does. The remarkable books published today, of which only a sample of references can be given in these pages, will stimulate the most reluctant to read, explore, experiment. Almost every book listed herein is illustrated.

Parents, teachers, and youth leaders will find it easy to guide the young readers to the suggested reading at the end of many of the 838 ways to amuse, as well as at chapter endings. All children have some special subject of interest (animals, dolls, space), and these are a start.

Teach them to use the index and table of contents, and going further, teach them to use the library for further exploring: the files, the bibliographies, and that most logical of locaters, the Dewey decimal system. Librarians are helpful but busy, and the following can make it easier and more fun: *Tell Me Some More*, by Crosby Bonsall, Harper (grades 1–3), full of fun but teaches library use as well.

There are many fine series of fact books by different publishers that encourage children to go back for the next volume. Among them are the following: Grades 1–3: *I Can Read* and *Let's-Read-and-Find-Out*, Harper, science; *A First Look At:*, Walker; *What Do They Do?* Books (policeman, cowboy, etc.), Harper.

Grades 1–5: *Books for Young Explorers*, National Geographic Society.

Grades 4–6: *American Indian Tribes*, by Sonia Bleeker, Morrow; *How Did We Find Out About . . .*, Walker, science; *Look & Make Books*, crafts; *American Folklore Series* and *Looking At* (other countries), all Lippincott; *Young Math Series* ("explore, understand and enjoy"), Crowell; and from Harper: *American Heritage Junior Library*, by the editors of *American Heritage, The Magazine of History, Portraits of the Nations, Horizon Caravel Books* (world history, culture, and arts, cave to the present), by the editors of *Horizon* magazine, and *Search for . . .* (. . . *King Arthur*, by Christopher Hibbert, . . . *Early Man*, by John S. Pfeiffer, etc.).

Education, we are told, is learning to use the tools that the human race has found indispensable. Do not let the size or seeming dullness of bibliographies intimidate the new explorer. He or she need only learn to use the index, under the field of interest sought, to find books on any subject on earth:

Children's Books: Awards & Prizes, Children's Book Council: includes the entire list of Newbery and Caldecott awards, National Jewish Council awards, regional and state prize-winners, and some books chosen by children.

The Best in Children's Books, Zena Sutherland, ed., University of Chicago: subject index includes literature on special subjects such as black Americans, Jewish children, American Indians, regions, and the handicapped.

The Arbuthnot Anthology of Children's Literature, edited by Zena Sutherland, Lothrop: the best books for all ages.

Children's Catalog (yearly), H. W. Wilson, and *Junior Literary Guild Books.*

Bibliography of Books for Children (a serial), Association for Childhood Education International: "a guide to quality," including fiction, biography, and nonfiction such as sports, drama, songs, and backpacking. Also, a series in paperback by the same group: helping the convalescent, cooking and eating with children, overcoming sex-role stereotypes, and a guide to children's magazines. See *Where Children Are Concerned,* for parents and teachers.

Notes from a Different Drummer: A Guide to Juvenile Fiction Portraying the Handicapped, by Barbara H. Baskin and Karen H. Harris, Bowker, annotated for the types of handicap, both mental and physical.

The Bookfinder, vol. 2, *A Guide to Children's Literature About the Needs and Problems of Youth Aged 2–15.* American Guidance Service: helps, through fiction, in solving problems ranging from adoption, appearances, ethnic differences, love, and school to working mothers.

Superintendent of Documents, Government Printing Office, Washington, D.C. 20402. Request a list of publications on the subject of interest (free).

Courage to Adventure: Stories of Boys and Girls Growing Up with America, compiled by Child Study Association of America, Crowell, grades 4–6: A salute to our bicentennial that will last until our tricentennial; stories of America's two hundred years: "will be read and reread, worthy of the home library."

There are other sources of reference—for example, dictionaries and encyclopedias, your local library and book store, and *Parents* magazine all will be of help in choosing the best books of the year. And on the very last page of this book is a final list of enticing subjects, broadly called "Understanding Our World," which includes one of today's foremost topics: mathematics.

All the above bibliographies are indexed and grade- or age-rated. However, do not be concerned if your child reads above or below the stated level. If he or she reads above, let the child go on the fast track. If below—well, your child is reading, so cheer him or her on. Only through reading will the child improve.

And finally, some helpful organizations and their addresses: Boy Scouts, Girl Scouts, and Campfire Girls, check your local branch; National Audubon Society, 950 Third Avenue, New York, New York 10022; National (and World) Wildlife, 225 East Michigan Avenue, Milwaukee, Wisconsin 53202 (publishers of *Ranger Rick,* rated one of the best children's magazines—check library lists for others); Sierra Club, 228 East 45th Street, New York, New York 10017.

With the help of any of the above, the family's shelves need not be filled with the assembly-line trash that outsells quality all too often because of lack of parental knowledge and discrimination. Families that possess several of these lists also can readily produce a practical suggestion for Grandmother or Uncle Rich at gift time.

CRAFTS

Families with school-age children often know the formulas and methods employed in the basic crafts.* They are, therefore, not repeated in this book. However, a number of suggestions are listed below to assure success with the various crafts discussed in this chapter:

GENERAL SUGGESTIONS

1. Always begin a craft plan by first reading the entire instructions, to be sure all necessary materials are on hand, and to form a general picture of what is to be done.

2. If heavy paper or cardboard is to be folded, lay a ruler on the fold line, run a blunt knife such as a table knife along this edge, then fold.

3. Rubber cement and white glues such as Borden's or Wilhold are among the best all-around adhesives for paper and cloth. Where taping is suggested, plastic tape is superior to cellophane tape if the object is to be kept for any length of time. It comes in both a natural tone and colors.

To set glue or paste on flat surfaces, place in a book under a weight or other books. The book can be protected by putting paper over and under the pasted item.

* If not, these can be found in *Home Play for the Preschool Child*, by the author, Harper & Brothers, 1957. They include many types of painting methods (finger, poster, sponge, soap, blot), potato printing, and directions for modeling dough and clay. In general, most of the painting discussed in this book is based on the inexpensive, easy-to-use dry poster paint from stationery and hobby shops.

6

4. To cut circles if no compass is available, use bottoms of glasses, cups, etc., or plates turned upside-down.

5. For large sheets of paper, use wide shelf paper or cut open a giant market bag. Glue several together if necessary.

6. "Craft" paper, also known as construction or art paper, is the term used in this book to describe the heavy sheets of many colors found in stationery stores or the five-and-ten.

7. Bristol board is excellent for paper furniture, cards, etc., and can be found in art or stationery stores. "Velour," a velvety paper, also in such stores, is expensive but can be used sparingly for frames, cards, etc.

8. Keep a box or drawer for craft supplies: paper rolls, boxes and cardboard of all types, corrugated wrapping paper. Other supplies to build up over a period of time:

FOR CRAFTS: (from hardware, stationery and five-and-ten stores): Plaster of Paris, white glue, tempera (poster paints) and brushes, clay, colored craft paper, a sheet of velour paper, crepe paper, newsprint, plastic tape, masking tape, various colors of enamel in five-and-ten sizes; fine picture-hanging wire, leather punch, spray cans of varnish or shellac, colored cellophane tape, sequins, small beads, glitter, Styrofoam, buttons, scraps of felt, rickrack, lace, ribbon. Use oil-cloth or plastic to protect work surfaces.

FOR THE DESK (from stationery, five-and-ten, drugstores): Writing board, cellophane tape, rubber bands, brass paper fasteners, paper clips, erasers of all kinds, crayons, scissors, ball-point pens and pencils (colors and black), large notebook, small pocket notebooks, notebook paper (lined for easier writing), gummed reinforcements, pencil sharpener, ruler, stapler, paper punch, India ink.

FOR SEWING: A sewing box (or make one, p. 50), sets of pins and rather large needles, small boxes for embroidery thread, thimble, basic colors of thread, scissors, yarn bits, buttons, cloth measuring tape, darning egg, all kinds of leftover scraps and materials.

FOR CARPENTRY: Not too heavy, but real rather than toy: hammer, small saw, screwdriver, pliers, steel measuring tape, square, vise, boxes or jars of nails, screws, and bolts in various sizes.

FOR REPAIRS: Household cement, plastic tape, plastic cement, glue.

PRACTICAL AIDS

Safe Razor for Craft Use

To make a double-edge razor blade safe for cutting, when a scissors is unsatisfactory, wind a strip of adhesive tape around both sides to cover the holes. Over one edge fold several thicknesses of tape to prevent cutting the fingers. This leaves one sharp edge exposed. Sharpen on carborundum from the five-and-ten.

Keepsake File

To make a file for keepsakes and other purposes, get a small carton, about 13 inches wide, at the grocery store (Fig. 1, A). Buy inexpensive manila folders from the five-and-ten,

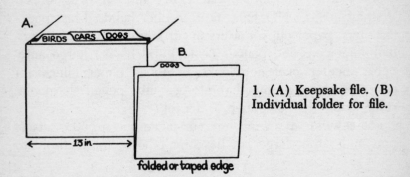

1. (A) Keepsake file. (B) Individual folder for file.

or make some of two sheets of cardboard or craft paper taped together along one side. If you make your own, make a tab that stands above the folder (Fig. 1, B), to label the contents (such as "My Stories," "Fourth-Grade Spelling Tests," "Patterns," "Space News").

File the folders alphabetically ("*Birds*," "*Doll Pictures*," "*Letters*"). Until the box contains enough folders to remain upright, place a brick or stick in the box behind the folders.

When you get a party favor such as a shamrock, drop it into "Patterns," to copy at a future date. Letters to answer will be on hand under "Letters." Snapshots or scrapbook pictures that have not yet been placed in a book will not get lost. You will find dozens of uses for a file.

Booklet Boxes

If you do not have a file, booklets, magazines, or completed school workbooks may become lost or get torn. Even with a file they sometimes become too bulky. For such materials, make a book box.

Cut two pieces of cardboard slightly larger than the largest booklet or magazine. Cut a 3-inch-wide top, bottom, front and back, as shown (Fig. 2). Use masking tape to tape the sides to the top, bottom and back.

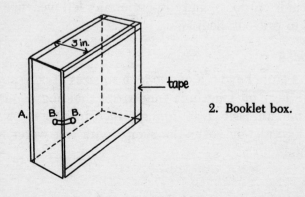

2. Booklet box.

Tape the front down one side only (A), for a hinged door.
Tape this one edge both inside and out, for strength.

Coat the entire outside surface of the box with glue or
paste, one side at a time, and then cover with wallpaper
scraps, wrapping paper, craft paper, or pieces of fabric. When
thoroughly dry, fasten a brass paper-clasp handle, or sew a
button to the opening flap, and another around the corner on
the side of the box (B). Hold fastener with a rubber band, a
small tape tie, or a ribbon.

Fill with booklets or other materials and place on the book
shelves.

MODELING AND SCULPTURING

Plaster of Paris

Purchase the dry mixture at a hardware store (around five
cents a pound). Estimate the amount of plaster needed, and
pour that amount of water into a clean food can. Slowly pour
powder into the water without stirring, until a small peak
forms above the water. This is enough of the powder. Then
stir, keeping the spoon under the mixture to prevent air
bubbles, which weaken it. Stir until the spoon leaves marks
in the mixture, and then pour immediately. To slow setting,
add a bit of vinegar; to speed setting, add a pinch of salt.

Wash hands outdoors, and dispose of any leftover mixture
there also to prevent clogging.

Papier-Mâché

Prepare a large bowl full of one-inch squares of newspaper
as follows: Tear off long inch-wide strips, holding as many
strips as you can easily tear through, then tear these off by
the inch. Completely cover the scraps with hot water and
soak overnight.

Next, squeeze out excess water. Add one cup of paste to every three cups of paper and mix thoroughly. For paste, use the proportion of ⅓ cup flour to ¼ cup water. To avoid a messy mixing job, you may place in a plastic bag and knead.

Clay

Dry clay and Dextrine for the following articles can be purchased in art or stationery stores. Follow package directions. Add Dextrine to harden clay permanently without kiln drying.

BOWLS:

1. Molded bowl. Hold a ball of clay in the left hand, or place on a work surface, in this case being careful not to stick it fast to the surface. Press with your thumb to make a hole in the center, and with your fingers on the outside guide the shape (Fig. 3, A). Continue pressing and shaping, turning it as you work, being careful to maintain the same thickness all the way around. The clay can be molded into a round or oval shape, a shell or free form.

2. Coil bowl. Make long rolls of clay about the thickness of a large crayon or fountain pen. Coil this round and round, curving it in the shape desired. When finished this can be left as it is, with coils showing (Fig. 3, B), or the coils can be smoothed into a solid surface.

CANDLEHOLDER: Make a round ball of clay and press a candle into the center. Carefully remove candle and permit clay to harden (Fig. 3, C). Or shape the clay with the fingers, making a rim around the bottom to catch dripping wax (Fig. 3, D). Or make a free-form base, following any shape you choose (Fig. 3, E). Paint with poster paint or enamel when dry.

HANDPRINT: Roll out a piece of clay ¼-inch thick and a bit larger than your hand. Place a plate over this and outline a circle, or make it slightly oval. Cut the edge with a knife

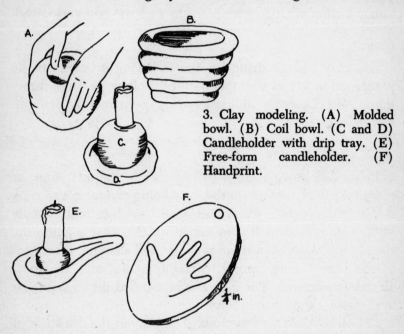

3. Clay modeling. (A) Molded bowl. (B) Coil bowl. (C and D) Candleholder with drip tray. (E) Free-form candleholder. (F) Handprint.

or a straightened paper clip, smooth the edge with a finger, and then press the hand into the clay. While still damp use a pencil to make a hole for a hanging ribbon (Fig. 3, F). Paint with enamel when thoroughly dry.

Soap Carving

Use a soft, large cake of soap, such as Ivory or Fels Naphtha. Leave unwrapped for twenty-four hours to dry. Create a design on paper first, something simple, without too many angles or curves.

To carve, use a paring knife, not too sharp. Work over

paper or a tray to catch carvings for household use later.
First slice away brand name and raised edges, as little as possible (Fig. 4, A). Trace the outline on the soap (B). Lay the
soap on a breadboard or other surface for the first cutting
and cut from top to bottom, removing excess soap (C).

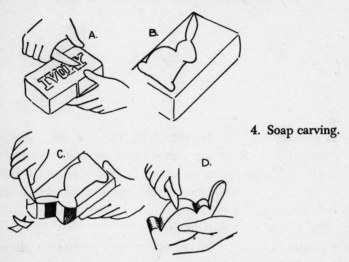

4. Soap carving.

For the general shaping of the piece, hold in the hand and
carve as in peeling a potato. Work all around the design
instead of doing one section, such as the head, first (D).
Work from the high points that stand out to the low points,
deeper in.

For finishing, smooth with the knife. Mark details such as
eyes with an orange wood stick or sharpened wooden lollipop
stick. Let set for a day or so to dry, then smooth *gently*, with
face tissue, fingers and palm of hand.

Cotton Modeling (Animals)

For this, pure white surgical cotton can be used, or the
cheaper cotton batting. Cut off a piece about 6 inches square

and roll from one corner diagonally to another, to make an oval ball. Paste the end down to prevent unrolling (Fig. 5).

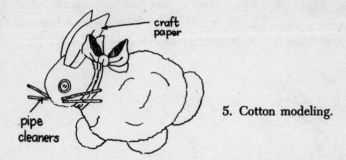

craft paper

pipe cleaners

5. Cotton modeling.

About one-third of the distance from the end, tie a pretty bow to form the neck of the animal and separate the head from the body. Shape a face with your fingers. Use bits of felt, paper or other stiff material for ears and tongue, or even eyes, or use buttons, beads or sequins for eyes, and paste on. Add a small bell to the ribbon if desired.

For legs and tail, shape bits of cotton and paste into place.

Sponge Animals

Cut pieces of sponge into the parts of the bodies of animals and cement together (Fig. 6).

6. Sponge animal.

Box Designs

Put aside every pretty, odd or interesting small box you find. Add leftover paper towel tubes, used gift-wrapping paper, scraps of cloth, and trimmings such as rickrack or lace. Collect pretty pins and buttons, beads, sequins, bits of bright felt, feathers.

Make animals, men, or abstract creatures of the boxes, and decorate with the other materials (Fig. 7).

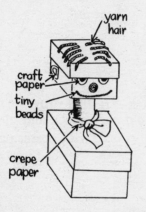

yarn hair

craft paper

tiny beads

crepe paper

7. Box design.

DESIGNS: PAPER AND PASTE, CRAYON AND PAINT

Stencils

A stencil is a design cut within a solid, unbroken frame, to be transferred to another surface.

Make stencil designs on heavy paper (see Fig. 8). The pear, shown, is the cutout area. Very carefully hold or pin the stencil to the paper or material to be decorated. Use poster or textile paints from a stationery store and fill in the cutout area completely on the paper or cloth background. Paint with a small brush, always working from the edge of the stencil to the open center of each design.

To cut a stencil, use a special knife from hobby or stationery stores, or make a craft razor (p. 8). Patterns may be Indian designs, (p. 108), fruits, flowers, vegetables, toys, etc. For a snowflake stencil, see p. 19. For uses, see "Rubber Tube Printing" below.

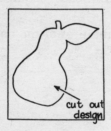

cut out design

8. Stencil.

Rubber Tube Printing

Make a paper pattern first (Fig. 9), then copy the outline on old rubber tire tubing. Cut out each piece and glue to a small board. Cover the tube pieces *only* with poster paint for

paper patterns   rubber tubing

9. Rubber tube printing.

printing on paper, or textile paint for cloth. Press carefully to the surface to be ornamented. Use for doll curtains, spreads and tablecloths, or for decorating cards or stationery.

Border Prints (Repeating Designs)

These can be used for putting an attractive border on the top and bottom of a tom-tom or knitting bag (p. 47). They can be used to form a border for a scrapbook, or to frame a picture, or to decorate doll houses (p. 66).

To make, cut a strip of gummed crepe paper or craft paper exactly as wide and long as needed. Fold into half (Fig. 10, A), then into thirds (B). Draw any design you wish (C),

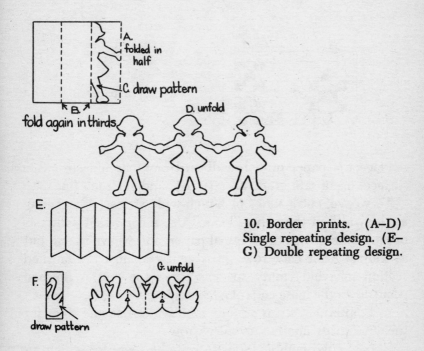

A. folded in half

C. draw pattern

B. fold again in thirds

D. unfold

E.

F. draw pattern

G. unfold

10. Border prints. (A–D) Single repeating design. (E– G) Double repeating design.

and cut, remembering only that *some part of each edge must remain uncut,* or the designs will fall apart when unfolded (D). The pattern may be geometric, dolls, trees, flowers, birds, boats, etc.

To make double designs, facing each other, fold the long strip of paper accordion-style (E), in the size desired. Draw a pattern on the top fold (F), being sure edges of the design touch each side, cut, and unfold (G).

Woven Paper

Draw lines the length of a sheet of colored craft paper, ½ inch apart and leaving a border of one inch on each end (Fig. 11).

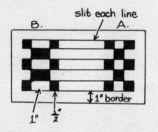

11. Woven paper.

Place the paper on a breadboard or other indestructible surface. use a safe craft razor (p. 8), and slit each line.

To weave, cut a series of ½-inch-wide strips (A), as long as the width of the paper "loom." Use a color that contrasts or harmonizes with the original paper, and weave in and out as shown. After *each* row, press gently against the finished section to avoid empty spaces. When the mat is finished paste down the loose ends of each strip.

In B, alternate strips are one inch wide. Use one color for the wide strips, another for the narrow.

Choose color combinations to suit the room for which intended. Use for table mats, small chest or dresser mats. These can be made any size. Glue several together if paper is not large enough. Make a miniature size for a doll house, using narrow strips.

Snowflake Design

Use a pencil compass or a small glass to cut a circle the size of the snowflake desired. Two inches across is a good size for a design (Fig. 12, A).

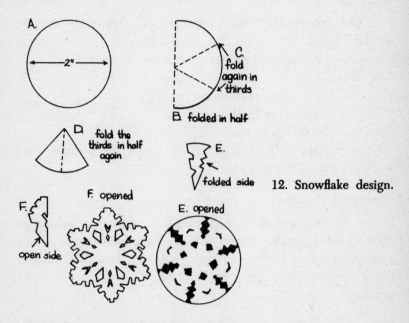

12. Snowflake design.

Fold the circle in half (B), then again in thirds (C), and fold the thirds into halves again (D).

If a stencil is desired, in order to transfer the snowflake design to another surface, cut as shown in E. *The main cuts are on the fold line.* This opens as shown in E, opened. The snowflake shown in dark background is within an unbroken circle. To use, see "Rubber Tube Printing," p. 16.

If a snowflake outline is desired, to be pasted to other surfaces, cut the main design *along the open edge* as shown in F, with the folded edge cut just once or twice to add interest.

This opens as shown in F, opened. Use snowflakes glued to colored craft paper for Christmas ornaments; use for scrapbook designs, border designs (p. 17), or paste in rows along the wall of a doll house for wallpaper.

Wallpaper Ideas

1. Cut designs from wallpaper scraps, glue to the corners of plain five-and-ten-cent-store mats, shellac twice.
2. Cover a wastepaper basket. Shellac if desired.
3. Make a set of paper-plate pictures (p. 34).
4. Use to decorate stationery (p. 49).
5. Cut designs for birthday cards.
6. Cover a booklet box (p. 9).

Stores where wallpaper is sold often have old samples they are willing to give away free.

Cut-Paper Designs

For creating a picture with designs cut from craft paper, choose, for a small picture, a 3-by-5-inch file card, or cut a circle of white cardboard using a large glass as a pattern. For a larger picture use a piece of craft paper for the background.

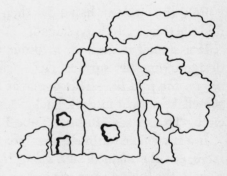

13. Cut-paper design.   14. Torn-paper design.

Draw the design first, the exact size of your planned picture. Make it simple, with easy cutting lines. Cut out each figure separately.

Trace the pattern pieces on colored craft paper and cut out. Glue these to the background rectangle or circle (Fig. 13).

Torn-Paper Designs

The same as above, but *tear* the shapes, very carefully, instead of cutting them (Fig. 14).

Shell Scene

Draw a scene and decorate with a variety of little shells. A shore scene is especially attractive. There could be blue water edged in sand, glued on, and sprinkled with groups of shells; perhaps also walks, roads, a little house, made of shell.

Cutout Pictures

Use a piece of heavy craft paper for the background. Thumb through magazines for interesting items that are in proper scale with each other.

When a fair collection is ready, lay the pictures out and see how many can be used to create an attractive scene. Do not make it too cluttered, and draw in anything lacking, such as sun, sky, grass.

Collage

A collage (rhymes with garage) is a solid picture made of small sections of many pictures, pasted together helterskelter to tell a story.

To make a collage, decide on a subject. Use mail-order catalogues or magazines to find pictures to suit. Any subject will do: a family, the city, crops, careers, transportation;

15. Joanne, Billy, and Rick, perched above a collage picturing "Vacation Days," are listening to a favorite sound of summer. (*Photo by Harold Hall, Van Nuys, Calif.*)

whatever appeals most. (For a vacation collage, see Fig. 15.) A collage of a family, for example, may show a house, partly covered by family members and their possessions, or family scenes such as watching TV or playing ball together. Each scene is small, perhaps oddly shaped, half-covered by another, giving glimpses or snatches that suggest the theme.

Collages are much more attractive when all or some of the pictures are in color.

Textured Painting

"Painting" with sawdust (from a lumberyard) creates an interesting texture. To prepare the sawdust, dye it (any except redwood or cedar) the color desired by covering with poster paint. When the color has soaked in, drain sawdust on newspaper and dry. Draw the outlines of a picture on a cardboard back. Then spread paste on all the areas that are to be a certain color: green, for example, such as grass and trees. Sprinkle the green sawdust on this. When dry, paste over the areas for another color, and repeat until the textured area has been covered color by color. For better contrast cover only part of the picture with sawdust; perhaps just the figure, in front of a painted or crayon-colored background. In this case, do the textured part last.

Variation: Experiment by adding dried coffee grounds or sand, plus a little glue, to small quantities of poster paints.

Textured Crayon Pictures

Draw a picture with crayons, and when finished use as many materials as possible to give texture to it. A scene of a boy with a bat, for example, could have a thin sponge "plate" beneath him, the bat a stick glued over the colored bat, the ball a flat circle of cotton of the thin layered type that comes in jewelry boxes. Clothes can be real fabrics glued on, but avoid porous materials such as linen, which shows the glue. Trees could be covered with tiny torn bits of green craft paper, glued on one over another like shingles. The possibilities for ingenuity are almost unlimited.

For another use for this see "Shadow Box," p. 168.

Crayon on Cloth

Use unworn sections of old sheeting. Color a master design on paper, copy on the material and color, pressing heavily with ordinary crayons. When finished place on news-paper, colored side down, and iron with a warm wet cloth and hot iron. Use for designing doll items: curtains, bedspreads, dresser runners, etc., or for costumes.

Crayon-Scratch Designs

Use many different colors of crayons to create a design (rather than a picture) on a smooth paper. Color over it solidly with black crayon. Open a paper clip and use this to scratch another design. This removes the black, permitting lines of color to show through.

Crayon-and-Paint Designs

Draw a design of interesting lines by pressing heavily with a crayon, and then paint over the whole picture with thin poster paint. Or, draw anything you wish on black construction paper and paint over it with white poster paint, or draw on white paper and paint with black paint.

Marbleized Paper

Use the edge of a scissors or a dull knife to scrape little chips of crayons of various colors onto a piece of paper. Cover with other paper and press with a rather hot iron.

Mosaics

A mosaic is a scene or design created by fitting together many small, varicolored pieces.

TILE MOSAIC: For this you will need: sixty-four ¾-inch tiles, in several colors, found in hobby or tile shops; grout, a very inexpensive filler found in hardware, plumbing supply or hobby shops; a good glue such as Wilhold; a 7½-by-7½-inch (8-by-8-inch will do) piece of thin plywood.

Create a de ign first, in crayon colors, on graph paper. An Indian desigr (p. 108) or any geometric pattern works well. When ready, begin at a corner of the plywood and work one row at a time, coating each tile underside with a layer of glue, and placing in position (Fig. 16, A). Tiles should be

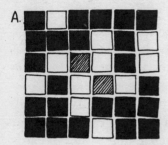

16. Mosaics. (A) Small tile mosaic (36 squares). (B) Punch-dot mosaic.

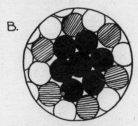

magnified punch dot
section

approximately ⅛ inch apart. Allow twenty-four hours to dry, and then reglue any loose tiles if necessary, again allowing time to dry. Now seal the edges of the plywood with adhesive tape, preferably the flesh-colored, shiny-finish type.

Mix powdered grout with water, adding a little at a time until a thick, whipped-cream consistency is reached. Pour carefully in the spaces between the tiles, pressing firmly until level with the tiles. Do not clean the tiles of the excess grout until it is fairly well set in the crevices.

Allow eight hours' drying time and then glue felt, or strips of felt, to the undersurface of the plywood.

This makes an excellent and attractive hot pad. A 4-by-4-inch size can be used as a drink coaster or under a vase.

PUNCH-DOT MOSAICS: Punch a number of dots from colored craft paper with a paper punch. The larger the hole, the easier the work will be. Keep the colors separate. Design a pattern using different-colored dots in lines, circles, diamonds, Indian designs (p. 108), etc. Making a pattern on graph paper makes any type of design easier to execute.

Cut a 4-by-4-inch square of white cardboard. Cover lightly with glue, a section at a time. With a pin lightly prick and pick up a dot of the proper color. Place in one corner of cardboard and work away from it, or in the center as shown in Fig. 16, B, until the square is complete.

Apply design to both sides for a mobile decoration. Or use as a wall ornament. Or shellac twice (let dry before second coat), and use as a coaster. Four coasters, all different in design, make an attractive gift.

BUTTON MOSAIC: Cut a square of cardboard, 4 by 4 inches or 8 by 8 inches as desired. Lay out old buttons in a design. If there are enough to make a solid pattern, cover the cardboard with glue and, following the laid-out design, place buttons in position. If there is a space between the buttons, first cover the cardboard with craft paper and then glue on the buttons. (See Index for other mosaics.)

DECORATIONS AND ACCESSORIES

To Wear

EARRINGS: Make earrings of stiff cardboard painted on both sides with nail enamel or other paint. They can be any unusual shape desired, and may be decorated with sequins, beads or glitter, glued on. Round earrings for pirates, gypsies, and so on can be made of cardboard covered with foil.

When finished, glue or punch holes near the top of the earrings. Through holes, attach a small loop of string that just fits the ear. Slip over the entire ear (Fig. 17, A).

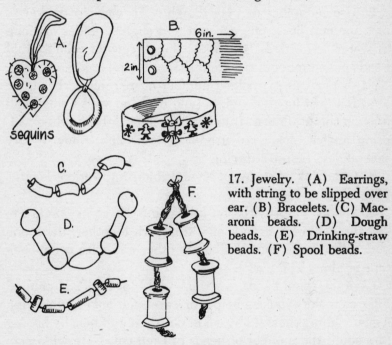

17. Jewelry. (A) Earrings, with string to be slipped over ear. (B) Bracelets. (C) Macaroni beads. (D) Dough beads. (E) Drinking-straw beads. (F) Spool beads.

BRACELET: Cut a 2-by-6-inch band of thin cardboard. Decorate with a design done in several shades of nail enamel or enamel paint. Or cover with oddly shaped bits of brightly colored gummed crepe paper, to create a mosaic design. This can be shellacked or covered with colorless nail enamel if desired (Fig. 17, B).

Fasten by stringing ribbon through two holes on each end, tying inside the wrist.

BEADS:

1. Make beads of elbow or shell macaroni. This can be colored if dipped quickly in and out of water with food coloring. When thoroughly dry string with cotton rug yarn, twine or shoestring. Stiffen the end of the string with glue or tightly wind with cellophane tape (Fig. 17, C).

2. Use modeling or play dough. (To make play dough, mix one cup flour, one cup salt and slightly under one cup of water as needed.) Color the dough several colors. Mold beads in a number of sizes and shapes to create interest (Fig. 17, D). For variety make a number of marbleized beads by kneading just long enough to hold together well a small ball of each color. Make a stringing hole in each bead while wet, using an ice pick, yarn needle or toothpick. Allow to dry several days before stringing.

3. Cut drinking straws of several colors into various lengths (Fig. 17, E).

4. Spools. Paint with non-lead paint. To string, braid (p. 97) three 40-inch strands of cotton yarn together; tie at one end with a large knot; stiffen the other end with cellophane tape or glue (Fig. 17, F).

Give the spool beads to a small child for a gift. If painted different colors you can help him learn their colors by playing a game, lining them up by color. Or teach numbers by having him count the number of beads of each color. He will enjoy stringing them himself.

YARN FLOWER: Cut a one-yard length of thick wool yarn or 18 inches of cotton rug yarn. Wind this on a loom made of heavy cardboard, ½ by 2 inches (Fig. 18, A). Tie ends together at the bottom when wound (B). Run a 4-inch length of green yarn through the bottom and knot firmly (C, D). Now pull gently from the loom and separate each looped strand of yarn at the top to form a circular flower (E). The green yarn is the stem. To make a corsage, make several flowers of different colors. If stiff stems are desired, wrap the green yarn stems around green pipe cleaners, using a small amount of glue.

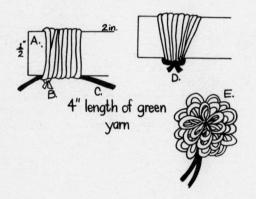

18. Yarn flower.

Use these flowers pinned to a skirt or blouse, or as a pony tail ornament, or on purses, cards, scrapbooks, or in textured pictures or shadow boxes.

For the Home

PETAL FLOWERS: Stick two sheets of gummed crepe paper back to back, or use one thickness of craft paper. Cut circles of different sizes, using drinking glass bottoms for patterns. Scallop the edges (Fig. 19, A) or fringe (B) by cutting toward the center with scissors. Glue a small circle of another color in the center. Curl the leaves as shown (C), over a knitting needle or matchstick. Glue a green crepe or craft paper leaf to the back.

Use on a mobile (p. 38), or on cards, or for textured pictures (p. 23). Or tape several in a group to a mirror for a party decoration.

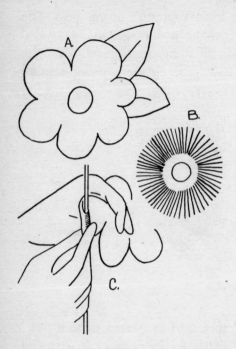

19. (A) Petal flower, made of a scalloped circle of craft or crepe paper. (B) Fringed flower. (C) How to curl flower edges over a small stick.

CARNATION: This is very easily made and looks real when finished.

Fold one doubled face tissue in half lengthwise, and accordion-pleat, about ½ inch for each pleat (Fig. 20, A). When pleated cut off the folded edge (B). Tie the center tightly (C) with picture wire, thread, or narrow ribbon.

There will be four layers of tissues on each side. Very carefully pull these apart, and the carnation is made (D).

For a stem, attach a garden "Twistem" wire to the tie at the center, or use florist's wire, green ribbon or green pipe cleaners curled by winding around a pencil.

For colored carnations use colored face tissue. Pink or white tissues may be very lightly streaked on the outer edges with nail polish to add variety and color. If desired the edges may be pinked, in step B, but this makes the pulling-apart somewhat more difficult.

Variation: Toilet tissue works equally well and also comes in color. Three double sheets, separated, laid one on top of the other and then accordion-pleated and tied, form a flower

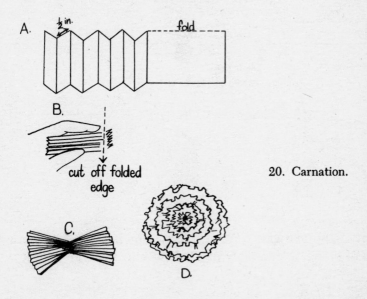

20. Carnation.

about the size of a face-tissue flower. For a miniature carnation lay two double sheets together, cut to any size desired, and accordion-pleat in ¼-inch folds. Toilet tissues cut in half lengthwise make a pretty miniature.

CREPE-PAPER FLOWERS: For a flower ½ inch in diameter, cut a piece of crepe paper ½ by 2 inches. Run a basting stitch as shown (Fig. 21, A), then pull the basting thread while pushing paper down to the knot (B). Twist the paper to form the flower (C), and run the thread back through again, knotting on the bottom (D).

This tiny flower can be used in textured pictures (p. 23) or on greeting cards. Use a piece of pipe cleaner for a stem. For a larger flower cut a wider strip.

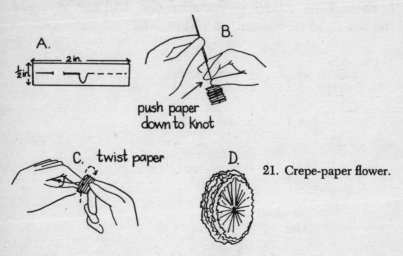

push paper
down to knot

C. twist paper

21. Crepe-paper flower.

PINWHEEL FLOWERS: For a ¼-inch pinwheel flower, cut a strip of crepe or thin craft paper 6 by ¼ inches (Fig. 22, A).

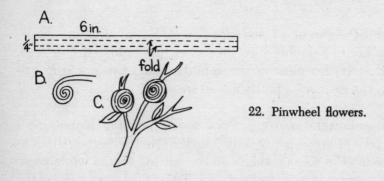

fold

22. Pinwheel flowers.

Roll or fold to make a long strip as thin as possible, and wind into a pinwheel, gluing the end (B). Draw the stem and

leaves, or cut slivers of green crepe or craft paper and paste
to background (C). Use for textured pictures or cards.

TULIPS: Cut the individual egg cups out of a molded egg
carton. Scallop the sides that are not already cut (Fig. 23, A).
Poster-paint the little cups in gay tulip colors.

23. Tulips.

Fill a cottage cheese carton with sand, gravel or soil, and
cover with silver foil. Make stems by bending pipe cleaners
down ½ inch and gluing to the cup bottoms. Push them into
the sand in a pleasing arrangement (B). Be sure the stems
differ in length. Leaves are made separately of green craft
paper stiffened with pipe cleaners or garden "Twistem" glued
to the backs.

THE FLOWER TREE: Make seven or more white carnations
(p. 30). With the lightest of strokes streak the edges with
red or pink nail polish.

Spray a deadwood branch white, and stand upright in clay
or Styrofoam. Cluster four flowers around the base; wire the
rest to the branches (Fig. 24). Place on a headboard or
dresser top. Replace the flowers when no longer fresh-look-
ing.

Variations: Use colored tissues to suit the room colors, or white streaked in gold or silver. Use the same deadwood branch for seasonal decorations such as Christmas ornaments, Easter eggs, Halloween craft-paper designs.

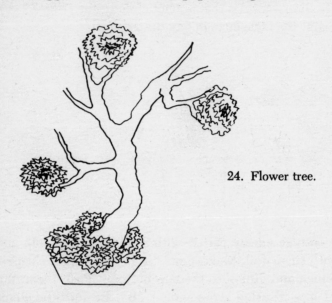

24. Flower tree.

Pictures and Frames

PAPER-PLATE PICTURES: Choose paper plates with fluted edges, or decorate the edges as described below. For the center, you can:

1. Color or paint a picture.

2. Cut a picture from a magazine and glue it in.

3. Use gift-wrapping paper or wallpaper, both of which often have beautiful subjects, scenes, or designs.

4. Cut designs from attractive cloth. Sometimes subjects from several materials may be grouped to form an original scene—perhaps a house from one scrap of cloth, a tree from another, a figure from still another.

5. Use pictures of friends or family.

6. Cut out different fabrics in the shape of hats, vests, faces, and create your own pictures (Fig. 25). Felt is excellent for this because it does not fray. Use large and small rickrack for eyes, mouth, bows, sideburns and whiskers. Use sequins for earrings, buttons or jewelry.

25. Paper-plate picture.

These plates can be left in the natural white, or painted with enamel or poster paints before the pictures are mounted, or just the rim can be painted to make a frame. For other framing suggestions, see "Picture Frames" below.

These pictures are most attractive when hung in pairs or grouped. Those with ribbon ties can be hung with cellophane tape or a very small nail. Others can be hung with picture hangers from the five-and-ten.

PICTURE FRAMES: Here are a number of suggestions for framing pictures and decorating the edges.

1. Fold bright-colored craft paper into three parts. Glue a picture into each section (Fig. 26, A).

2. Cut two strips of craft paper 11 inches long and 2 inches wider than the height of the pictures you wish to frame. Glue or cellophane-tape the two strips together as shown (B). Beginning at the taped fold (see arrow), meas-

ure off a section two inches wider than the pictures to be framed. Accordion-fold from the taped middle, working each direction, as shown. Cut off any excess paper at the ends. Glue a picture into each section. Tie with a ribbon to carry in purse (C).

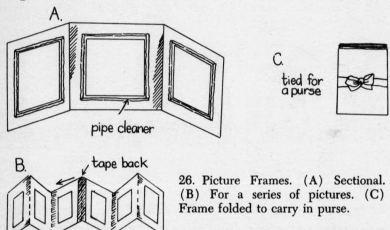

26. Picture Frames. (A) Sectional. (B) For a series of pictures. (C) Frame folded to carry in purse.

3. Glue a picture to heavy cardboard, about an inch larger than the picture all around. Cut a piece of craft or velour paper, burlap, felt, or other interesting material the size of the cardboard. Cut an oval, rectangular or circular hole in the material and glue to the cardboard to frame the picture.

4. Frame a picture with a doily, cutting a suitable hole in the center. Glue to colored craft paper if desired. Tie a ribbon to the top for hanging.

To decorate the frames of these pictures, or the "Paper-Plate Pictures" above, use one of the following suggestions:

1. Make holes every ¼ or ½ inch all around and lace a ribbon in and out, tying at the top with a bow (Fig. 27, A).

2. Glue a continuous edging of lace, rickrack, or velvet ribbon around either the picture or the frame.

3. Glue wee shells around the picture itself, or the outside edge of the frame.

4. Use a pipe cleaner in a color that contrasts with the frame—white on red, for example (Fig. 26, A).

5. Sponge-paint the border.

6. Frame with a border print (p. 17) made of white paper for a colored frame or colored paper for a white frame.

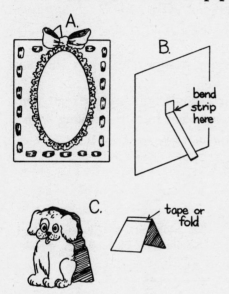

27. (A) Ways of decorating a picture frame. (B) Cardboard strip glued to the back of a picture to permit standing. (C) Stand-up pictures for use in a game.

To make frame stand, cut a strip of heavy cardboard, ½ inch wide and one inch longer than half the height of the picture. Bend strip as shown (Fig. 27, B), glue to frame, and extend behind picture.

STAND-UP PICTURES: Cut out any magazine pictures that might be used in a game: people, furniture, cars, houses, etc. Paste these on cardboard and lay under a heavy object to dry. Then cut the cardboard to the shape of the picture, and a second cardboard exactly like it. Connect these at the top with cellophane tape, open at the bottom, and the picture will stand alone (Fig. 27, C).

Variation: The same idea can be used with crayon pictures. Fold a piece of heavy paper, and then draw the picture to the top of the fold. Cut the paper to the outline of the picture, being careful *not* to cut the folded top edge. The picture will then stand alone (Fig. 27, C).

Mobiles

A mobile is a freely hanging design that moves with any breeze.

The very simplest type is a single light-weight craft item, such as a bird or flower, suspended from the ceiling with a thread. Other mobiles:

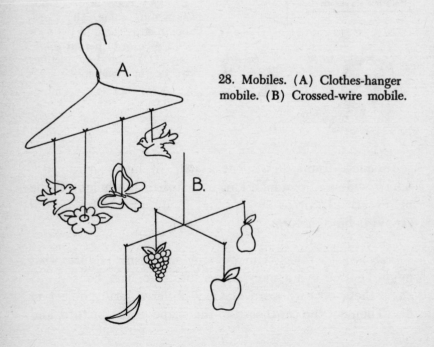

28. Mobiles. (A) Clothes-hanger mobile. (B) Crossed-wire mobile.

WIRE CLOTHES HANGER: Hang four or five ribbons or threads of varying lengths from the wire, each holding an object (Fig. 28, A).

CROSSED WIRE: Twist one wire at right angles to another and suspend an object from each corner, all at different, balanced lengths (B).

TRIANGLE MOBILE: Cut five wires in the following lengths (Fig. 29, A): (1) the spiral, 18 inches; (2) 36 inches; (3)

A.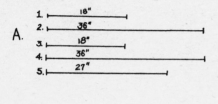

B.

C.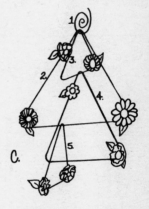

29. Triangle mobile.

18 inches; (4) 36 inches; (5) 27 inches. These can be wound with strips of crepe paper if desired. Form the top spiral; bend wires into thirds (B), hook over one another as illustrated (C), close triangles by wiring together with picture wire or covering with more crepe paper. Hold in the proper positions with picture wire.

To decorate any of the above mobiles, use birds below, paper flowers (p. 29), papier-mâché fruit (p. 10), craft paper decorated on both sides or any other light-weight, pretty objects. They can be made seasonal by using paper eggs at Easter, ornaments at Christmas.

Hang the mobiles by suspending from a light fixture, a screw in the ceiling or a beam, or from a bracket extended from the wall.

Birds

1. To make a decorative bird, draw pattern on graph paper, using Figure 30 as a model. Cut out wings (A) and

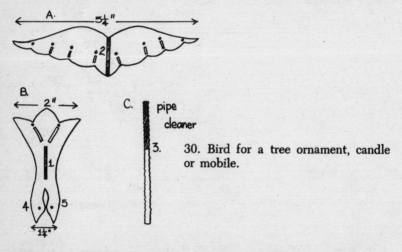

30. Bird for a tree ornament, candle or mobile.

body (B) of felt, thin layers of Styrofoam, foil, or craft paper. (Foil can be curved into the most realistic shape but will hold better if stapled where glue is suggested.)

Staple or glue the darkened area of the pipe cleaner C-3, *under* the darkened area A-2. Staple or glue B-1 *over* A-2. If glued, set aside to dry. When ready, glue B-4 to B-5. Use very small beads or contrasting bits of foil or other paper for eyes. Run lines of glue along the small outlined rectangles on the wings (A) and tail (B) and sprinkle with sparkle. Shake off excess. If desired, glue sequins where dots are shown.

Leave the long end on the pipe cleaner to attach the bird to a mobile (see above) candle, or Christmas tree.

2. On graph paper draw the body, wings, and tail of the bird shown in Fig. 31. Then transfer design to craft paper. Color in the eye. Moisten the edges of the tail, wings and

31. Bird for party decoration or mobile.

beak with glue and sprinkle with glitter. Cut a slot just behind the head (Fig. 31, A), to insert wings, and staple or glue firmly. Cut tail slot (A), insert tail and glue to position.

Hang several of these from a mobile (see above), flower tree (p. 34), or the Christmas tree, or use as spring party invitations. To suspend from a mobile, attach a thread to the body behind the wings (D).

Stained-Glass Medallions

Save up colored cellophane from candy wrappings and elsewhere. When several colors have been saved, use a compass or a plate to draw a 6-inch circle on black craft paper. Cut out circle and use a sharp craft razor (p. 8) to cut designs in the circle. The black areas shown in Fig. 32 are the uncut black background remaining. Use the pieces cut away as patterns to cut the different colors of cellophane, but cut each cellophane piece ⅛ *inch larger than the pattern* all the way around. Cover the black background with glue and glue the cellophane over the openings.

32. Stained-glass medallion. Each section is a different color of cellophane or tissue paper.

Hang in a window where it will catch the light, or give as a gift. The medallion can be cut in the shape of a cross, a diamond, a triangle, etc. Colored tissue paper may be used instead of cellophane.

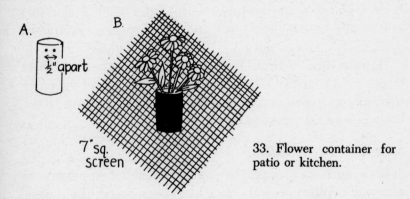

A.

½" apart

B.

7″ sq. screen

33. Flower container for patio or kitchen.

Flower Container

Cut a 7-inch square of window screen, paint it and a frozen-juice can the same color: Black, or one that suits the area where it will hang. Punch two holes in the can near the top and about one-half inch apart (Fig. 33, A). Turn the screen so that it has a point on top and looks diamond-shaped. Thread wire through holes in can and wire the can to the screen. Hang on a wall and fill with flowers (B). It should be removable to permit emptying the water.

Wall Bowl of Fruit

Buy a small individual wooden salad bowl at the five-and-ten or supermarket. Make miniature fruits of papier-mâché (p. 10) or clay (p. 11). While still wet, insert stems made of bits of twig, wire covered with gummed green crepe paper, or florist's wire saved from corsages. Paint fruit with poster paints when dry.

34. Wall bowl of fruit.

Glue these firmly to the bottom of the bowl in a pleasing arrangement (Fig. 34). Three or four leaves can be tucked behind fruit if desired. Make these of gummed crepe paper glued back to back, or craft paper.

If preferred, long wire stems can be attached to the fruit

while still soft, and these can be caught together and the entire bunch of fruit glued in as a unit.

Attach a picture hanger to the back of the bowl and hang in the kitchen or breakfast room.

Free-Form Wax Designs

Use old candles or paraffin. If there is not enough color, add wax crayons. (To be sure crayons are wax, scrape with the nail. Wax will curl off in chips.) Heat candles and crayons until melted, then pour a thin layer of wax into an individual pie or tart tin made of foil. (These are more easily managed by young children. Older children can manage full-size tins.) Let cool about one minute, then dip the tins of wax in a tub or plastic pool. (It is preferable to work outdoors with this.) Hold hands and elbows well *out*, not *up*, or wax will spurt up the arm.

When the tin is pushed into water rapidly, the wax billows suddenly into "sails." When done slowly it forms into rounded moons. These are lovely forms for use alone in decorating, or with flower or natural arrangements.

Decorated Bottles

SMALL: Soak off the label from a pretty bottle such as pills or household supplies sometimes come in. Use nail polish to paint the name of a spice, cake decorating item, sugar substitute, etc., on one side (Fig. 35).

Paint a pretty all-over design or a border of spidery lines. Or paint a wide bright line around top or bottom.

LARGE: Have ready a number of dried egg shells broken into many small pieces. Choose a nicely shaped bottle. Paint with enamel of any color desired—perhaps a color that would look well in the living room as a vase or decoration or in the bathroom with bath salts. While still wet, sprinkle all over with eggshells, or carefully press them on in a design (Fig. 36).

Variation: Cover bottle with flat paint (indoor wall paint), and while wet carefully add sequins, beads, small pretty buttons, or sparkle. Or use rickrack, cotton, bits of felt or foil, or any other decorating material. Have the materials ready

| 35. Small decorated bottles. | 36. Large decorated bottle. |

ahead of time, and before beginning draw a simple design on paper to follow in general as you work. A common pin is helpful in placing the small decorations.

If the bottle has no stopper take it to the five-and-ten before decorating and find a cork to suit. Paint to match the bottle and then decorate it, or cover with glue and decorate. Use a funnel to fill with bath salts.

Pencil Holder

A frozen-juice can covered with yarn makes a pencil holder for desk or telephone. Cover the top inch of outside of can with glue and wind yarn row by row, being sure each is close to the previous row. Add more glue and yarn until finished, changing colors if desired (Fig. 37).

37. Pencil holder.

Vase

Find a pretty jar, such as honey or jams often come in. Cover with a design, using several colors of thick poster paint chosen to harmonize with the room for which the vase is intended. When dry coat with shellac, if desired, for permanency.

Enamel paint or several shades of old nail polish may be substituted instead.

Decorated Containers

Use small-size round oatmeal boxes or ice cream cartons. First, measure the carton up to the lid (shown by arrows, Fig. 38, A). Cut a piece of bright craft paper or wrapping paper as wide as the arrows indicate, and as long as the circumference of the box. Cut a matching strip to fit the side of the lid (small arrows), and a circle to fit the top. To do this turn lid upside down and draw around, then cut about $\frac{1}{16}$ inch inside this line. Carefully paste these pieces on the box, smoothing out air holes.

If plain paper is used, decorate with a border print (p. 17) or paint a design if desired.

For a string holder, cut a small round hole in the top. This

box can be used also as a container for gift cookies or
candies, or for yarn or sewing items.

Variation: Make a knitting bag by using a large oatmeal
box and fastening a handle as shown in Fig. 38, B.

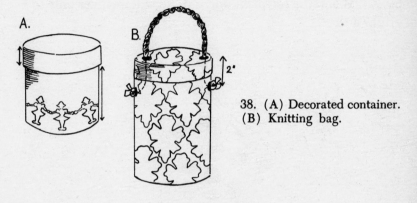

38. (A) Decorated container.
(B) Knitting bag.

GIFTS TO GIVE

In addition to the suggestions below, many of the items
described elsewhere in this book make excellent gifts. See
in particular "Toys of Paper and Paste," p. 77.

Surprise Ball

A surprise ball is one package made of strips of crepe
paper and holding many small surprises. These can be individually wrapped if desired.

To make, leave crepe paper folded in the package and cut
off 2-inch strips. Start with four strips, in differing colors if
possible, adding as many as needed. Lay out about ten or
twelve small items, to suit the person for which it is intended:
gum, wrapped penny candy, miniature cars and men, dolls or
furniture, jacks, pencils—anything small. Start with the long-
est item. Wind this in a strip of crepe paper until covered.

Add the bulkiest items next, by laying one at a time beside the wrapped items, wrapping each in turn with the crepe windings. Cellophane-tape wherever necessary to hold strips in place.

When finished it will look like a crepe-paper "ball" (Fig. 39, A). When the recipient opens it, he will uncover only one gift at a time.

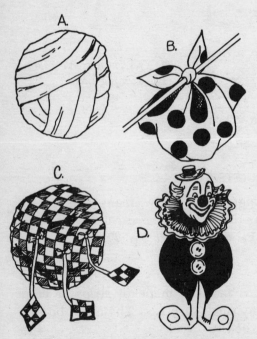

39. Surprise balls.

If desired, the finished surprise ball may be decorated.

Wrapped in a bandana and attached to a stick (B), the ball could be used as a hobo party favor or going-away gift.

The checked surprise ball (C) is filled with trinkets and wrapped in a little tablecloth made of a square yard of checked material, and tiny matching napkins are used as decoration. It could be given to a girl convalescent with the trinkets wrapped in different colors of crepe paper and instructions to unwind only one color each day.

The clown (D) could be a boy's birthday gift. The head is cut from an old birthday card. Shoes are made of cardboard, colored black execpt for "holes," and bent at the instep.

For other Surprise Balls, create a decoration using pictures from old cards or magazine pictures stiffened with cardboard.

Decorated Stationery

Buy plain white notepaper at the five-and-ten. Cut small designs from scraps of cloth and glue to a corner of each piece (Fig. 40).

40. Decorated stationery.   41. Paperweights.

To make a fine gift for someone with an autumn birthday, cut small designs from old Christmas cards and glue to stationery.

Paperweights

Use scraps of flannel or woolen material, and a pinking shears if available. Make a paper pattern. This can measure approximately 5 inches both ways, but can be shaped like a circle, a butterfly, a car, etc. (Fig. 41). Using the paper pattern, cut two designs if the material is heavy, three or four designs if light. Stitch these together firmly in the middle, slipping a rock in between before stitching closed.

Basket Purse

Buy a plain small wicker or straw purse at the five-and-ten. Decorate it with small shells, beads, or old artificial flowers or fruits that can be separated and used individually. Choose colors to suit the clothes to be worn with it. Plan a design first on paper, and use household cement or white glue to place decorations.

Sewing Box

Get a wooden cigar box at a drugstore, pull out the inside lining and soak off the label with a warm damp cloth—not too long, or the wood will warp.

Choose for a lining a sturdy material that will not show soil (oilcloth, plastic, awning material, denim). From this cut a strap 2 by 4 inches to strengthen the lid. Fold the strap lengthwise and stitch the edges under. Glue to lid and side as shown (Fig. 42).

Measure the sides of the box accurately and cut pieces of lining material the exact sizes of front, bottom and back. Glue into the box and bind the corners with gummed plastic tape to match the material. Be careful not to go over the rim or the box will not close tightly. The lid lining should end ¼ inch from the front edge and ⅛ end each side for the lid to close tightly. If you have no plastic tape, cut the linings ¼ inch larger all around, glue hems under or stitch on the machine, and then glue to the box.

Paint the outside of the box with enamel, using one of the colors of the lining. Decorate the lid with pipe-cleaner letters spelling the recipient's name, or bits of felt cut in a design, or shells, or anything else desired. If felt is used, designs could be sewing symbols: scissors, buttons, spools, etc.

For a spool rod, measure the exact inside width of the box. Use a piece of doweling this length and ¼ inch thick.

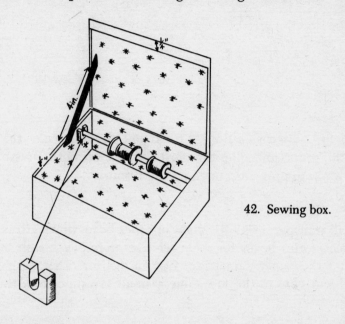

42. Sewing box.

Hold in position with two erasers or tiny blocks of wood glued one inch from the top. One eraser must have an opening cut from the rod hole of the eraser to the top, to insert the rod (see Fig. 42).

Fit this box with small boxes for pins and buttons, embroidery thread and the like.

Jeweled Box

Use a little plastic box, the colorless, transparent type such as many items come in. Glue sequins, fake jewels (may be

taken from old earrings), pipe cleaners, or shells to the lid
for decoration (Fig. 43). Plan the pattern first on paper.

If soaking the box removes the advertising paper but not
the glue, cover the same area with an attractively shaped
piece of bright-colored felt. This can be decorated as above.

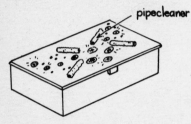

pipecleaner

43. Girl's or woman's jeweled box.

If it is to be used as a dresser ornament choose a color that
suits the room, and glue tiny strips of felt on both ends of
the bottom to prevent scratching the furniture.

Accessories Box

Small transparent plastic cigar or other boxes make attractive accessories boxes for male relative or family members.
Soak off the paper nameplate. Cut an oval or other design
of felt and glue to the top. Glue a small toy pipe from the

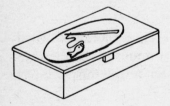

44. Boy's or man's accessories box.

five-and-ten, or any other masculine ware, to the felt. Or
glue other colors of felt, cut in the motif of a favorite sport
(Fig. 44). Line with scrap flannel, felt, velvet, or a layer of
cotton. Glue two strips of felt to the bottom to protect furniture.

Plastic Purse Envelope

This is for carrying all the miscellaneous lists, receipts and extra cards that will not fit into a card holder or wallet, or for purse face tissues. Choose a plain plastic bag approximately 5 by 10 inches. Tape a one-foot ribbon along one side of the top, extending out on either side. Use nail enamel or enamel paint to paint a design on the bag. To hold contents securely, fold the top back down and tie the ribbon around the bag. Decorate with sequins if desired.

Garden Ties

Cut nylon pantyhose along the seam, then into one-inch strips. These stretch and will not injure the plants. Use for tying climbing roses, chrysanthemums, sweet peas, and so on. Package attractively. If desired, these could be stuffed into an Accessories Box (p. 52).

Doorstop

Cover a brick with oilcloth. Use a color that suits the room, and blanket-stitch (p. 121) the edges with a contrasting color. Cut designs from patterned material and glue on.

Book Ends

For a pair of heavy book ends, cover two bricks with felt, using a blanket stitch (p. 121) in a contrasting color. Make designs with other colors of felt, and glue on (Fig. 45).

Highway Torch

Save twelve half-gallon or quart milk cartons. Completely open one carton at the top by removing the staple that holds the lid.

Cut the tops and bottoms from all the other cartons, fold

them and stuff into the first carton. Give as a gift for a safety torch to keep in the car for changing a tire or other highway stops at night.

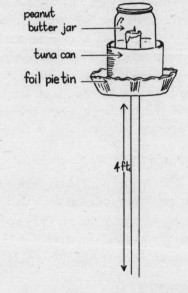

45. Felt-covered brick book end.   46. South-Sea outdoor light.

South-Sea Outdoor Light

Use a 4-foot length of doweling or old broomstick. Whittle the rounded end to a point and nail a tuna can to the straight end. Paint can and stick. Insert a large-size peanut-butter jar, or any other that fits equally well, into the tuna can.

Hold a lighted match near the bottom of a short, fat candle. When a bit of wax has dripped into the center of the jar, set the candle into the soft wax to hold in position. Give as a gift for an attractive yard light for entertaining.

Variation: If desired, flute the edges of a large foil pie tin by bending with the fingers. Paint the bottom and nail to the stick *under* the tuna can (Fig. 46).

Litter Bag

Use a *heavy* plain plastic bag approximately 8 by 12 inches. Tape a loop of ribbon about 6 inches long to one corner of the top. Tape all edges, for strength. Colored cellophane tape or plastic tape is fine for this. Paint a design using household enamel or nail enamel, or tape a design—perhaps Sparky, the Litterbug kangaroo.

Give as a gift to hang in the car, for holding trash.

HOUSES AND DOLLS

Paper House

Cut an 8- or 8½-inch square of paper. Fold in half along line 1 (Fig. 47, A), in half again along line 2. Open; refold

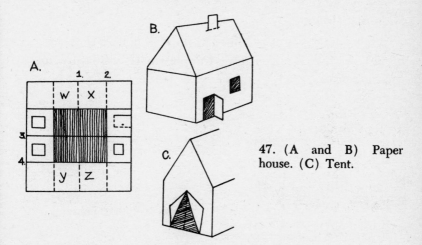

47. (A and B) Paper house. (C) Tent.

very lightly along lines 3 and then 4. Cut dotted lines as shown.

Color the four center "roof" sections, drawing in the direction shown. Cut out the windows (shown as squares) with a small nail scissors or craft razor (p. 8), or just color them. Cut the door along the dotted lines only.

Now fold square *x* completely over square *w* and paste. Fold square *y* over *z* and paste, and the house is finished (B). To make a chimney, cut a very small slit across the roof top and insert a small square of red paper.

To make a miniature house for a tiny scene or diorama (p. 167), use a 4-inch square of paper.

Tent

To make a tent, follow directions given in Fig. 47 for a house, but omit coloring the roof. Leave out windows, door and chimney. When complete, cut a vertical slit through the pasted square *wx;* fold back for an opening (Fig. 47, C).

For another tent, see p. 83.

Shoe-Box House

When small houses are needed for doll houses or to create miniature towns, farms, etc., for play with miniature men, use shoe boxes.

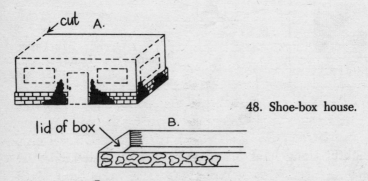

48. Shoe-box house.

To make, turn upside down and cut the bottom of the box around the three dotted lines as shown in Fig. 48, A, for a hinged roof to permit placing of furniture and dolls or men. Glue the top rim of the box, now the base, to the lid (B), or tape it on the inside with plastic or adhesive tape. Color the sides of the lid to resemble bricks or field stone.

Cut windows and doors on dotted lines. Paint the box with poster paints or house paint. Paint the roof a contrasting color if possible. Glue tiny sprigs of lichen or spagnum moss, from a hobby shop or the woods, to resemble plants coming up from the brick or stone base, or cut small bushes from green paper and glue on. Follow suggestions given under Carton Doll House (p. 65) for inside and outside window frames, walls and floor.

Shoe-Box Village

This village can be easily packed away in a carton, with church, school, and peaked-roof types on top.

Follow general suggestions given for a shoe-box house, above, but vary for these buildings:

JAIL: Cut strips out of one side for bars (Fig. 49)

CHURCH OR TEMPLE: Turn the box with an end for the front. In this end cut an arched door; cut arched windows on the sides; color or paste small "stained glass" windows (p. 41) in their place. Cut a slit in the roof just large enough to hold a little cardboard cross, or firmly glue a small box to the roof, and paste on it a cross or Star of David (Fig. 50).

SPANISH-STYLE HOUSE: Paint the box white or brush with a thin layer of plaster of Paris (p. 10) after it is made. Insert popsicle sticks or old-fashioned wooden clothespins split lengthwise into the sides near the top (Fig. 51), painting brown or leaving the natural wood color, to resemble beams.

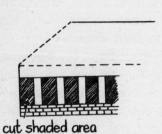

cut shaded area

49. Shoe-box jail.

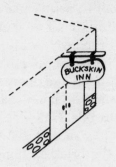

52. Shoe-box inn.

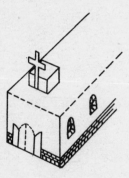

50. Shoe-box church.

53. Grocery store.

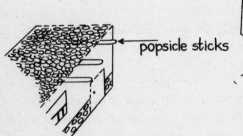

popsicle sticks

51. Beamed Spanish house.

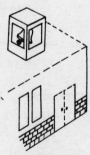

54. Schoolhouse.

These should stand out from the house about ¼ inch. The beams from the front can be taped or glued to those from the back where they meet inside the house, if desired, to give strength. Glue tiny strips of black to the lower halves of the windows to resemble iron grills as shown. Coat the roof with white glue or household cement brushed on, then cover with small gravel. If plaster of Paris is used, press in roof gravel while plaster is wet. Let dry thoroughly.

INN: Glue or tape a popsicle stick to the inside of the hinged roof, so that it will jut out over the street as in Fig. 52. Paint if desired. From this tie two strings, or thin leather thongs (p. 114), and a small board or cardboard. This can be cut into any special shape, such as an animal head, and should have a name (such as "The Stag," or "Buckskin Inn") as shown.

GROCERY STORE: Print a name across the front, up near the roof. Cut a wide double door, paint in a long window with fruits, vegetables, etc. (Fig. 53). If preferred, this could be a general store, as in frontier days. Inside, small boxes can be placed on their sides or glued into position to form counters.

SCHOOLHOUSE: Give this building double doors and many windows. On the top glue a little box with the upper part of each side cut out (Fig. 54), and a little bell hanging inside.

RANCH HOUSE: Follow procedure in Fig. 55, A. Cut both ends (1) from a shoe-box lid. Bend sides (2) up. Score with a knife and bend lengthwise along the center line (3). When finished, the lid (house roof) will resemble Fig. 55, B.

Now cut one side (6) from the box (see Fig. 55, C) and cut the removed side in half lengthwise along line 4.

Use plastic tape to fasten the lid sides (2) flat to the top of the box (5), creating a roof (Fig. 55, D). Tape half of the cut-off side (6) to one edge of the roof as shown in D. This creates a porch. Tape the cut-off ends of the lid (1), shortened to the proper length, to the porch roof as pillars (7).

To store away, fold porch under.

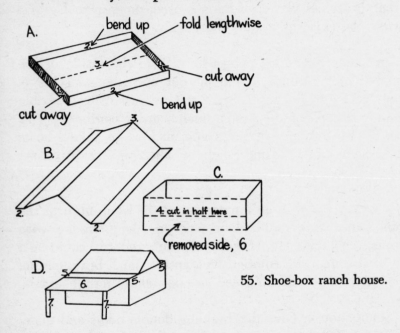

55. Shoe-box ranch house.

BARN: This requires twin shoe boxes in order to obtain two lids.

With each lid, cut off the ends (1) as in Fig. 56, A. Bend one side up (2). The lids are taped firmly together on the remaining side (3), creating a high roof as shown (Fig. 56, B).

Cut one side from the box bottom (Fig. 56, C), leaving one inch around the upper and side borders to avoid weakening the box (4).

Securely plastic-tape the roof to the box at four points (5).
Barns are traditionally painted red, or red and white. For
corrals, see p. 90.

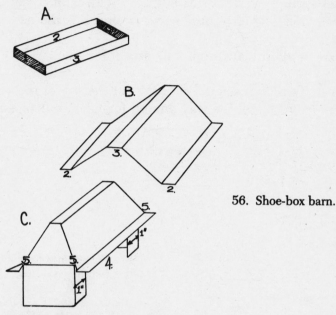

56. Shoe-box barn.

Shoe-Box House Furnishings

BEDS: Make of papier-mâché (p. 10). For box beds, a small
matchbox with lid removed is the right size for miniature
dolls, but miniature men need pillboxes or toothpick boxes.

To make legs, cut the ends from four matches, push
through the corners of the box, extend to ¼ inch below the
bottom, cut off even with the top of the box, and glue (Fig.
57, A).

For a headboard, cut a piece of cardboard the exact width
of the box and twice as high and glue into position. Paint
or paper entire box, or cover headboard with a scrap of
pretty fabric glued on. (See Doll House, p. 65.)

MATTRESS: Cut a piece of old sheet that is *twice as wide* as the box-plus-½-inch, and just as long as the box-plus-½-inch. Fold lengthwise. Stitch inside out along end and side, leaving one end open. Turn right side out, stuff with a bit of cotton, turn the remaining edge inside and stitch across the end.

PILLOW: Follow mattress pattern except for size.

SHEETS: Two pieces of old sheeting cut the size of the bed, plus one-half inch all the way around for hems and tuck-in.

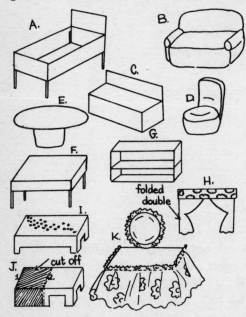

folded double

cut off

57. Furnishings for a shoe-box house. (A) Bed. (B) Couch. (C) Bench. (D) Chair. (E and F) Tables. (G) Bookcase. (H) Curtains. (I) Coffee table. (J) End table. (K) Dressing table.

BLANKETS: Small scraps of wool or felt. These can be buttonhole stitched around the edge if desired (p. 121).

SPREAD: A piece of pretty material cut the size of the sheets and hemmed. If it is to be tucked under the pillows, add ⅛ inch to the length.

COUCH: Make of papier-mâché (p. 10) or clay, and paint (Fig. 57, B). Rub excess paint off if clay is used. A padded seat and back can be made by covering with a thin layer of cotton (peeled from jewelry-box cotton) and gluing material over this.

BENCH: Make of clay or papier-mâché, or cut a small matchbox in half lengthwise (C). Paste on a cardboard back and paint or cover with a scrap of cloth or plastic.

CHAIRS: Make of a round piece of clay or papier-mâché, big enough to hold a miniature man, with a thumb-indentation for the seat, and a barrel-shaped back (Fig. 57, D).

TABLES: For a round dining table with one center (pedestal) leg, use clay or papier-mâché (Fig. 57, E). Make it tall enough for a seated toy figure. Make four armless barrel chairs as above.

For a rectangular table, use clay or papier-mâché, or a small matchbox turned upside down with matchstick legs glued to the inside of the box (Fig. 57, F). Paint any of these.

BOOKCASES: Several small matchboxes may be cut as for benches, above, but glued or taped one on top of the other (Fig. 57, G). For books cut cardboard rectangles small enough to fit on the shelves, glue three or four of these together to give thickness for each "book," and paint different colors.

CURTAINS: Cut bits of fabric double (Fig. 57, H), so that when folded and glued together at the top, the curtain will look pretty both inside and out. Glue to window frames. A valance may be made if desired by gluing a narrow strip of material above the window, covering the tops of the curtains also.

DISHES: Mold tiny dishes of clay, or make foil dishes by shaping foil around the end of your finger and flattening the bottom.

COFFEE TABLE: Cut out the sides of a small matchbox (Fig. 57, I). Paint. When dry decorate with punch-dot mosaics (p. 26) for a "tile" top.

END TABLES: Use lipstick boxes or a matchbox cut in half or in fourths (Fig. 57, J), with the cut-off side (1) glued or taped at the double-dotted line (2). Decorate to match the coffee table if desired.

DRESSING TABLE: Use a lipstick box or other small box, or cut down a small matchbox as for an end table, above. Cut a scrap of cloth as wide as the height of the dressing table and 8 inches long. Baste and gather into a ruffle, then glue to the top rim of the box for a flounce (Fig. 57, K). For a mirror, see p. 72.

CHESTS: Follow instructions on p. 68, using small matchboxes.

KITCHEN APPLIANCES: Make of clay or papier-mâché and paint.

BATHROOM APPLIANCES: Make of clay or papier-mâché and paint.
See also "Doll-House Decorations," p. 72, for the following: centerpieces, mirrors, lamps, indoor potted plants, pictures, mobiles, light fixtures, rugs.

Carton Doll House

Needed: three (or four if preferred) *sturdy* cardboard cartons. Those shown (Fig. 58) are apple boxes, approximately 16½ by 11½ inches. For a roof use a heavy cardboard clothing box opened out as shown, or two sides from other

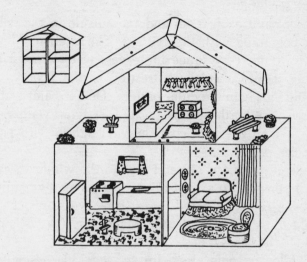

58. Grocery-carton doll house. *Kitchen:* Refrigerator is a baby-shoe box with a twine handle knotted inside. Stove is a shoe box cut in half. Counter is a long box with a hole cut the exact size of a smaller box, which is taped underneath for a sink. *Living room:* Chair is the end of an oatmeal box, with a back cut from cardboard. Pillows for seat and back are glued on and match couch cover. *Bedroom:* Dressing table is made of a cream carton with pleated skirt, and cardboard kidney top glued on. Stool is a spool with a bit of cotton covered by cloth tied with a thread.

cartons, approximately 16 by 12 inches each, hinged at the peak if necessary with adhesive, masking or plastic tape. If four boxes are used, each roof section should be approximately 24 by 12 inches.

Fasten the boxes together with brass paper fasteners (indicated in Fig. 58 as small dots), punching holes with an ice pick or nail. Attach roof in the same manner, but not until box tops are painted. Cut windows and doors with a heavy knife. Windows may be covered with Saran Wrap or cellophane if desired, then framed with ¼-inch width of white paper (see kitchen).

Poster-paint each room and the outside in the colors desired, beginning with the ceilings. The kitchen's "linoleum" floor is attained by squeezing excess water from a sponge, dipping it into a color contrasting to the floor color, and pressing lightly in a regular pattern. Do not paint walls to be papered. Use border prints (p. 17), or scrap wallpaper, first using a small brush to coat the wall lightly with paste (to make, see p. 11).

Make curtains (p. 71) and glue to the windows, as in the kitchen, or glue to a wall to cover a pretend-window, as in the living room, or gather on a string with brass fastenings to hold it, as in the bedroom. Make rugs (p. 73) and glue lightly to the floors if desired.

Paint lower roofs green for terraces. Place small potted plants or bushes around (p. 72) and make a garden bench by gluing popsicle sticks to spools as shown. (Popsicle sticks can be cut in half for back supports with heavy kitchen shears.)

Simplified Carton Doll House

From the grocery store get a canned-goods carton that has the top cut around three sides only, making a hinged roof through which to place the dolls. Doors and windows may be just painted on. Follow shoe-box house (p. 56) or carton doll-house ideas for completing it.

Simplified Doll-House Rooms

If you wish to make most of the furniture described below for a carton house, or most of the shoe-box furniture described on p. 61, decorate the insides of several boxes, either carton or shoe size, as individual rooms instead of houses, to allow more space.

Doll-House Furniture

This furniture is suitable for grocery-store carton doll houses (p. 65), or wooden houses.

BED: Glue four spools to a baby's or child's shoe box for legs (Fig. 59, A). Cut away all but two inches of the sides. Cut away half of the footboard end. Leave the other end as

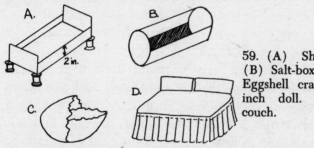

59. (A) Shoe-box bed. (B) Salt-box cradle. (C) Eggshell cradle for one-inch doll. (D) Studio couch.

it is for a headboard. Paint entire bed. Cover the headboard if desired with plastic or fabric. If a padded effect is wished, first glue a thin layer of cotton to the headboard.

For mattress and bedclothes, see p. 62.

CRADLE: Cut away half of the side of a salt box (Fig. 59, B) leaving ends as they are. Paint and decorate with ruffled netting, or cover with material glued on. Pad headboard as

described under "Bed," above, if desired. Place a layer of
thick cotton across the bottom before adding mattress and
bedclothes (p. 62). If desired one-third of the whole box
may be left, to create a hooded top.

Variation: To make an eggshell cradle for miniature doll
babies, break one egg in half lengthwise, one in half in the
usual way. Glue one of the latter into one of the long halves
(Fig. 59, C).

STUDIO COUCH: Turn a child's shoe box upside down. Cover
the bottom with a layer of cotton. Cut two pieces of material,
one inch larger all around than the box bottom. Lay one of
these on the cotton padding, then glue down the sides, turning the corners neatly as with sheets on a bed, and gluing
firmly.

Now cut a strip of the seat material thirty-six inches long
and as wide as the box is deep. Glue or stitch pleats at regular intervals (see "Curtains," p. 71), and glue around three
sides of the box (Fig. 59, D).

Go back to the second piece of material cut to match the
seat. Cut this in half lengthwise. Fold each half and stitch
inside out around three sides. Turn right side out, stuff
with cotton or strips of nylon hose, stitch the end, and you
will have two bolster pillows to prop at the back of the studio
couch.

DRESSER CHESTS: Glue two or three large matchboxes, with
the lids on, firmly together, one on top of the other. Paint
with heavy poster paint or enamel. Glue a button or wooden
bead to the middle of each, for a false drawer-pull. These
boxes really can be used for drawers but must actually be
pushed open from the end. (See doll-house bedroom, Fig.
58.)

DRESSING TABLE: Use the bottom of a large matchbox or another of similar size. Cut out one side. Turn upside down. Paint the top or cover with paper. Cut a 20-by-2½-inch piece of material and sew a ¼-inch hem all around. Leave the ends of one length open for a drawstring. Run a string through this hem by attaching the string to a yarn needle or small safety pin. Gather material to 10 inches and fasten to matchbox with brass paper fasteners. (See p. 72 for mirror suggestions; see also doll-house bedroom, Fig. 58.)

END TABLES: Cut away part of the sides of two large matchbox bottoms. Paint or cover with punch-dot mosaics (p. 26).

COFFEE TABLE: For a rectangular table, follow end-table suggestions. If a long table is desired, place two boxes end to end. For a round table, use the bottom of a round powder box or a third of a round oatmeal box turned upside down and painted. If desired, part of the sides may be cut away. (See doll-house kitchen table, Fig. 58.)

COUCH: Turn a small shoe box upside down and make a couch seat and sides as for the studio couch, p. 60. Cut a 2½-inch-high piece of cardboard and fasten across the back with brass paper fasteners. Pad thickly with cotton, stretching it over the top. Make a cover, pillow-case style, leaving one of the long sides open, and allowing an inch larger than the cardboard back all around because of the cotton. Carefully slip over the back, gluing at the bottom.

PILLOWS: Use a drinking glass to draw outlines for two small circles of cloth. Stitch together wrong-side-out, leaving an opening to insert cotton stuffing. Turn right-side-out, stuff, stitch opening. Sew a matching button exactly in the center, pulling down tightly to cause the rest of the pillow to puff.

Make a 2-inch-square pillow in similar fashion. If couch material is figured, the pillows should be plain, for contrast.

BOOKCASES: Turn two or three large lidless matchboxes, or others of similar size, on their sides, and glue firmly together, making open shelves for books or knickknacks. (To make books, see p. 63.)

CUPBOARD: For a small size, use a 6-inch Easter egg carton. For the shoe-box size, use a standard egg carton, not the molded type. Cut off the top two sections, being careful to leave a ¼-inch margin in order not to destroy the next sections (Fig. 60, A). Cut off the center peaks (2), and cut away the upper half of the remaining lid. Glue the lid flap down (3), both inside and out. Slit the lid through the center, making two doors. Paint the cupboard. Sew two buttons on as handles, or use two brass paper fasteners. Set far enough apart so that a small rubber band or thread loop can hold them closed when not in use. (For another doll cupboard, see p. 88.)

DINING TABLE: Use the bottom of a 3½-inch-square jewelry box turned upside down. Break or cut four popsicle sticks to 3-inch lengths. Glue these, broken ends up, inside the four corners for legs. When dry, paint. (For a round, oatmeal-box type, see the doll-house kitchen, Fig. 58.)

CHAIRS: Follow suggestions on p. 63. For the square table, chair seats should be about 1½ inches high. Or use a heavy kitchen shears to cut 1-inch lengths of popsicle stick. Glue two lengths to a spool. Make backs as shown in doll house, Fig. 58.

CURTAINS: For pull-back curtains, see p. 63. For informal draperies, cut strips of the material used for the couch, or use strips of netting, or old shirts or sheeting. Gather at the top and glue to both sides of the windows. A valance as described on p. 63 may be used.

For easy pleated curtains, cut a piece of material the length desired, and two and one-half times the width. Lightly

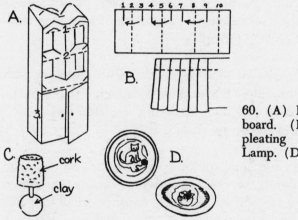

60. (A) Egg-carton cupboard. (B) Method of pleating curtains. (C) Lamp. (D) Lid pictures.

pencil-mark every ½ inch as shown (Fig. 60, B), and fold line 3 to line 1, line 6 to line 4, 9 to 7, and so on, stitching about ¼ inch from the top as you fold.

For informal curtains, leave pleats unpressed (doll-house kitchen, Fig. 58). For formal "draperies," press pleats the entire length (doll-house living room).

For gathered curtains (doll-house bedroom) cut the length desired *plus* ½ inch and stitch a hem across the top. Run a string through this and fasten to brass fasteners at each end.

Doll curtains need not be hemmed, but if this is desired, add ½ inch to the length in cutting.

Doll-House Decorations

CENTERPIECE: Press a bit of heavy foil, or a doubled light piece, into a one-inch bowl. In this, place very tiny fruits of painted papier-mâché or painted clay, for a table centerpiece. Or make a flat, rectangular dish of foil and "float" (without water, of course) wee crepe paper flowers (p. 31).

MIRRORS: For a dressing-table mirror, or for a wall ornament, use a round or oval tin lid from a cocoa can or similar type. This can be framed with tiny rickrack or lace, or a small velvet ribbon can be glued on.

LAMPS: Use corks, painted or covered with material, with matchstick stems and a clay base wide enough to balance the lamp (Fig. 60, C). For floor lamps for a carton doll house, use lollipop sticks and larger corks.

PICTURES: 1. Glue small pictures from a magazine or designs from material, or crayon drawings, inside aluminum milk-bottle caps, or soft-drink bottle caps, or small can lids (Fig. 60, D).
2. Cut small rectangles or circles of cardboard, rim with craft paper or rough material for a frame, and glue in a magazine picture or a crayon drawing.
Glue pictures to the doll-house walls in groups of two or more and about two inches from the floor.

PLANTS AND TREES: For indoor or terrace plants, make small pots of aluminum foil, soft-drink bottle caps, or corks. Glue, tape or just push "greenery" into these depending on the type. The greenery can be spagnum moss or lichen from woods or hobby shops, crushed green tissue, or artificial Christmas greenery from the five-and-ten.

For a potted tree, use the lid of a wide-mouthed chili bottle or something similar. Cover with foil, fill with real soil or clay. Use a twig for a stem and a green top as for the potted plants.

For winter trees, use small-branched leafless twigs. Base in a small mound of clay, papier-mâché or plaster of Paris.

A paper tree can be made of green craft paper by cutting four 2-inch half-circles, folding in half and then cutting these like a palm tree (Fig. 61, A), an evergreen (B), an oak (C),

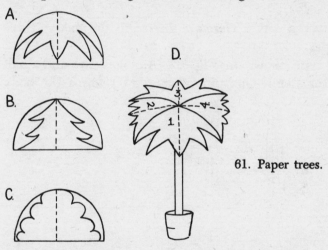

61. Paper trees.

or any other. Glue the four half-circles together at outer edges as in D. When dry glue the four-sided tree to a sucker stick or twig, and make one of the bases or pots described above.

RUGS: Braid rugs (p. 97) to suit the rooms of the doll house, or make woven paper mats (p. 18). They may also be made of any scrap of material cut in the size or shape desired. The doll-house bedroom rug (Fig. 58) is a rectangle fringed by cutting in one inch on the ends.

MOBILE: Make a miniature crossed-wire mobile (p. 38) and suspend miniature flowers from it (p. 29).

LANTERNS: Miniature lanterns make charming modern light fixtures. Suspend from thread taped to the ceiling.

Dolls

(For a doll suitcase, see p. 81. For a doll hobby, see p. 101.)

PIPE-CLEANER DOLLS: Here are directions for making three simple types.

1. The type shown in Fig. 62, A, takes two-and-a-half pipe-cleaner stems. One pipe cleaner (B) forms the body

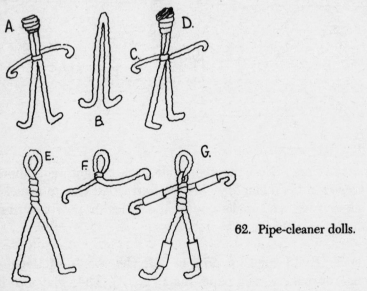

62. Pipe-cleaner dolls.

and legs. One (C) forms the arms, wound around the center to form the chest. One-half (D) is wound for the head. Cover with a bit of a different color for a hat, glued on if necessary.

2. Begin as in (B) above. Twist, leaving a loop on top (E). Loop arms and head (F) in through the loop left in (E). The finished figure (G) has soda-straw bits covering arms and legs to make them seem more natural.

3. Make a figure as in (1) or (2) above, but double the length by joining two pipe cleaners at the top, making a larger figure. If preferred, Chenille Craft, special long pipe cleaners found in hobby shops, may be used, in which case one would be enough. Make a head of a bead, or attach a small Styrofoam ball (purchased in packages at the five-and-ten). Use sequins, beads, or common pins for features. For hair use yarn, darning cotton, or a new wire pot cleaner.

ORNAMENTAL SPOOL DOLL: A quaint little spool doll can be made with four large spools (Fig. 63, A). Paint three spools a pastel color and glue together. Glue sequins, beads, or sparkle in a pattern. Glue the unpainted spool on top, pencil in a face, then paint. Attach yarn for hair by gluing one layer on top of another until desired thickness. Place a small paper flower (p. 31) or a sprig from an old artificial corsage in the hair. Use as a gift or a dressing-table ornament.

FOIL DOLL: Lightly crush one piece of foil into the size and shape of a medium potato for the body. Crush another into a ball half that size for the head. Make twenty grape-size balls: four for each arm, five for each leg, one flattened ball for each foot. Wire all together (Fig. 63, B).

Make eyes and nose with beads or sequins held with common pins. Use red nail enamel or a sliver of red cellophane tape for mouth. Give him a small beanie of red crepe or craft paper, or a pointed stocking cap made by twisting paper into a cone. Tie a bit of ribbon at the neck for a scarf, make buttons, and belt if desired, of red nail enamel, cellophane tape, sequins, or felt.

Use for a Christmas ornament, a trinket gift or doll collection.

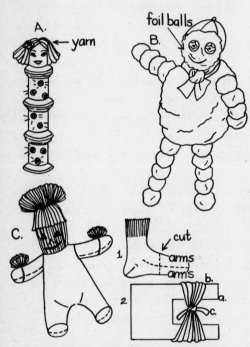

63. (A) Spool doll. (B) Foil doll. (C) Sock doll. (C1) Method of cutting sock. (C-2) Yarn tassel on loom.

SOCK DOLL: Patterns for beautiful sock dolls may be found in all pattern departments. The following one (Fig. 63, C) needs no pattern:

Choose a child's sock, size 8, perhaps red, with white wool-yarn for trimming and black embroidery for features. Cut off half the foot, as shown (1) and cut this piece into two arms, stitching the sides and stuffing with cotton or small strips of old nylon hose, then stitching the tops closed.

Slit the remaining part of the foot to within 2 inches of the back of the heel, to form the legs. Turn inside out and stitch, closing "toes" and inside seam.

Stuff entire stocking up to 1½ inches from the top, where it must be tightly tied. Sew on the arms, tie the neck, embroider the face. Turn the top down for a hat. Stitch a small pompon (below) to the top and a very small one to each arm, at the "wrist."

YARN TASSELS: For a head pompon for the doll above, or for doll clothes or doll curtains, make a 5-by-1-inch loom of heavy cardboard, cutting about ⅛ inch of the middle as shown in Fig. 63, C (2a). Wind a 3-yard strand of yarn around the cutout end (b). Tie the center (c), and gently remove from loom. Ends may be cut or not as desired. For a full-size tassel for dress or belt ties, clown pompons, or pinning to curtains, make the loom 5 by 3 inches and use a 10-yard strand of yarn. For the wrist tassels of the doll above, use a loom 5 by ½ inch with 18 inches of yarn.

TOYS OF PAPER AND PASTE

Boats

PAPER BOAT: The boat illustrated in Fig. 64 floats, and if made with waxed paper will last quite a while, but is too light for cargo, except possibly a small pipe-cleaner man.

Any size of paper may be used but must be square. An 8-by-8-inch square will make a boat about 6 inches long.

Fold to a triangle (Fig. 64, A, B). Fold point (1) to point (3), then point (2) to point (3) as shown in B. Carefully hold together the two half-flaps (1 and 2) with the *top* flap of (3), and fold back to (4). Now fold the remaining flap (3) back on the other side, making a triangle (C) that opens

like a cone (D). Fold (5) and (6) together to make a small
square (E). Turn the (5) and (6) section upside down and
pull apart the flaps of (7), shown in F. This opens to the
finished boat (G).

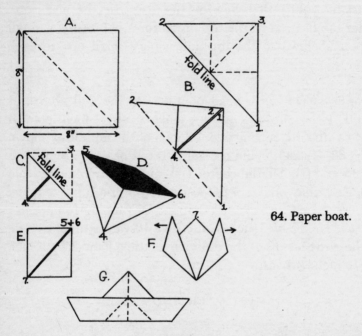

64. Paper boat.

INDIAN WAR CANOE: Use a piece of craft paper 5 by 8 inches
for an 8-inch canoe (Fig. 65). For a miniature canoe use a
3-by-4-inch sheet. Fold the paper lengthwise, then lightly in

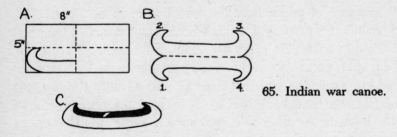

65. Indian war canoe.

half the other way (A). Draw half of a canoe, cut out and unfold (B). Glue or tape the rounded ends together (1) to (2), (3) to (4). Hold apart at the center with a matchstick with the tip broken off (C). This also forms a seat.

WALNUT BOAT: Use a half shell of a walnut, or a split peach stone. Push a one-inch length of toothpick through a tiny triangle of paper, for a sail. Drop a blob of glue into the boat and prop sail in this until set, or use a very tiny ball of clay stuck fast (Fig. 66).

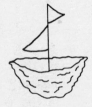

66. Walnut boat.   67. Bottle-cap boat.

BOTTLE-CAP BOAT: Attach a sail (made as for the walnut boat above) to the cork inside a soft-drink bottle cap or a waxed milk cap (Fig. 67).

BOX BOAT: Cream or milk cartons of any size make long-lasting boats. Press in the pouring spout and cut out one side. Push one end out slightly to form a prow. Glue foil to the sides to cover advertising (Fig. 68).

RAFT OR BARGE: Make as for box boat, above. The sides may be cut down if desired. Use white glue or plastic tape to attach popsicle sticks to the bottom as balancers. To fasten barges together follow suggestions for train attachment, p. 87, making holes above the waterline (Fig. 68).

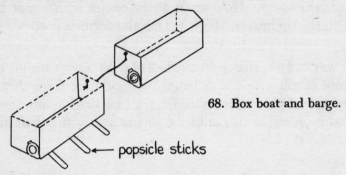

68. Box boat and barge.

← popsicle sticks

Circus Wagon

Paint a shoe box with lid a bright color. When dry cut openings in the sides, using a craft razor (p. 8), to provide the bars for the cage (Fig. 69). On one end (the back of the wagon), cut a door to place animals in the cage. Use a brass paper fastener as a handle. Opposite it in the wall of the

69. Circus wagon.

wagon, place a second fastener. Hold the door closed with a loop of thread or a rubber band stretched between the fasteners. Use a drinking-glass bottom or pencil compass to draw circles, and cut wheels. Also cut a cardboard handle. Paint these a contrasting color—yellow, perhaps, if the wagon is red. Attach wheels with brass fasteners. When finished, lid may be glued on if desired.

Suitcase

Tape one side of the lid of a shoe box to the bottom (1) as in Fig. 70, A, using a heavy tape such as plastic or adhesive. Tape the inside also by opening the lid fully when the outside is taped, and then taping the inside line. This is the hinged lid. If a sturdy box with lid attached can be found this step is saved.

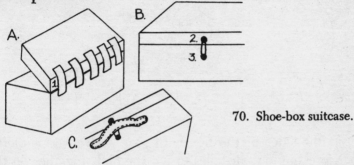

70. Shoe-box suitcase.

On the suitcase front punch two small holes (2) and (3), as shown in B. Insert brass paper fasteners to close the suitcase, hold finger under fastener (2) to permit closing. To hold the suitcase closed, wind thin string around the two fasteners; unwind and place in the suitcase to prevent losing it when not in use. Large, strong rubber bands will hold the suitcase shut if preferred.

For a handle, cut a piece of heavy cloth, 2 by 10 inches, fold lengthwise and stitch the three open sides under. Attach this to the suitcase front with two brass fasteners on each side for strength (C).

Piggy Bank

Remove spout from a salt box. Cut a slit in the side of the box large enough for coins. The slit will be the top (Fig. 71).

Measure the length and circumference of the box. Cut a piece of paper this size. Use wrapping paper in a small all-over design. Cut two circles of the same paper the size of the round ends. Double another bit of the paper over and cut two double ears, gluing back and front together, or use gummed crepe paper from the five-and-ten.

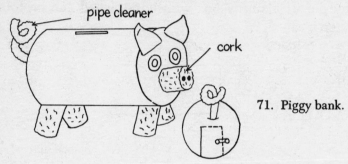

71. Piggy bank.

Coat the sides of the box with glue and cover with the paper, pressing out air holes; bring the ends together on the side opposite the slit. Cut the slit through the paper covering.

Glue the ears to the front circle of paper, and then glue it into position, pressing firmly. Curl the ears slightly with fingers or around a pencil or matchstick.

Glue on the back circle. Use a pencil to wind a pipe cleaner for a tail, then push this through the back of the box. Make eyes of notebook reinforcements or circles of white paper. Cut the end from a large cork to shorten it, and paint it and four other corks, or cover with the paper. Cut two round circles of plain dark paper, or make with a paper punch, for nostrils. Glue nose and legs into position.

If you wish to be able to remove the money easily, cut a little door on the dotted lines as shown below the tail. Use a brass fastener for a handle, fasten another opposite it on the box, and run a loop of thread or a rubber band around both fasteners to hold door shut.

Stand-Up Animals

Color, or cut from magazines bright animals and paste them on cardboard. Use spring clothespins for legs (Fig. 72, A). They can be used as table favors and decorations for

72. Stand-up animals.

a party. Or make small cardboard animals, give them stiff legs, with feet bent as shown, and use in the circus wagon (B).

Tent

Use khaki or green cloth if possible, although any scraps will do. Cut a rectangle 6 by 3½ inches. Cut a piece of cardboard 6 by 5 inches. Plastic-tape the long ends of the cloth to the long ends of the cardboard leaving a ¾-inch margin on each side. This gives the cloth enough leeway to place two

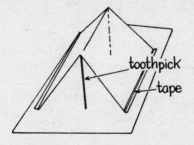

73. Tent.

toothpicks, one at either end, in the center as tent poles (Fig. 73). Enough of the toothpick may be broken off to stand upright, blunt end up to prevent puncturing cloth.

Use for hiking games, camping, etc. To store, remove toothpicks and pack flat. (For another type of tent, see p. 56.)

Stretcher

For a stretcher for miniature men, use two straight twigs about 3½ inches long. Toothpicks or matches will do but are a bit short. Glue a strip of cloth 3 by 3½ inches to each twig, winding one full turn.

Helicopter

To make a whirlybird that flies, see Fig. 74. Use a 7½-by-3½-inch piece of heavy craft paper, and cut as shown (A). Fold wings as shown and fasten the lower folds with a paper clip, to give weight (B). Drop straight down from a height of four feet or more, and it will whirl as it falls.

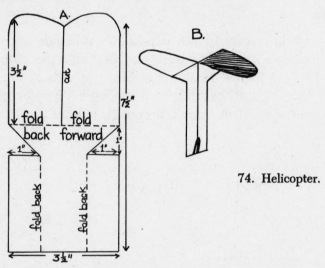

74. Helicopter.

Wallet

Fold an 8½-by-11-inch piece of paper in half (Fig. 75, A) along line (1). Then fold in the side borders (2) one inch each, resulting in B. Turn the top border on the unfolded edge (3) down one inch (B). Finally fold all this in half once more (C), along line (6).

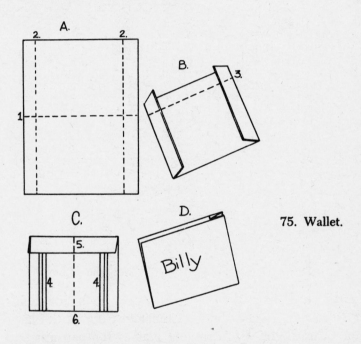

75. Wallet.

Draw a design or write name on the outside. Seal flaps on both sides (4) with tape or glue. To open, lift flap (5). The result, D, is fine for play money, trading cards, etc.

Train of Boxes

To make, use shoe boxes, small cartons from the store, or matchboxes large or small, depending on the size train

desired. Shoe stores usually have extra boxes they will give
away.

ENGINE: To make a shoe-box engine, find two boxes, one
just enough smaller to fit snugly inside the other. For the cab,
cut away about ⅓ of the smaller box (Fig. 76, A). Cut holes
in the sides for windows. Insert the larger section of the

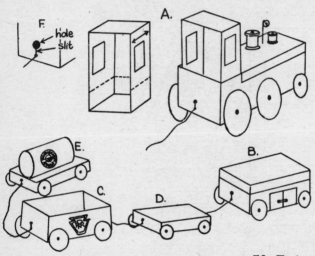

76. Train of boxes.

smaller box upright in the bigger box, with open side facing
back as shown. Attach a brass fastener in front of the large
box for a headlight. Use drinking glasses for patterns, cut
six disks from cardboard and attach with brass paper
fasteners for wheels.

Now measure the depth of the cab box, as shown by the
arrows in A, and cut away this amount from the large box
lid. Glue or tape the lid to its own box, in front of the cab, as
shown. Glue two spools into position for smokestacks. Glue
or tie two matchsticks together and tie on a small bell.

This engine is large enough to carry men, dolls, or animals. If wheels are not fastened too tightly, they will roll.

BOX CARS: Use boxes with lids for box cars (Fig. 76, B). Cut doors in the sides large enough to insert toys. To hold doors shut, use brass fasteners on the doors far enough apart to be held with a small rubber band.

GONDOLAS: Lidless boxes (Fig. 76, C).

FLAT CARS: The lids left over from the gondolas (Fig. 76, D).

TANKERS: Oatmeal or salt boxes glued to shoe-box lids (Fig. 76, E).

Tie cars and engine together with heavy string. To permit uncoupling, punch a small hole for the string. Cut a narrow slit from this hole up to another hole large enough to permit knot to slip through (Fig. 76, F).

To add more realism these can be painted with poster paints, but this should be done before assembling. Paint different names, symbols, and slogans on the sides, similar to those on real trains. (See also "Hobbies," p. 126.)

MATCHBOX TRAINS: Either large or small sizes may be used. With these, turn the box upside down for the engine. Glue about ⅓ of the cover to the top for the cab, after cutting out windows.

The large matchbox train is best for bed play.

African Native Hut

Measure the circumference of a brown paper bag, one that is around 18 inches or so. Cut a piece of corrugated packing paper (or other stiff paper) 3 inches high and as long as the bag is round, plus ½ inch for stapling.

Staple, plastic-tape or glue ends of corrugated paper together, rough side out and standing vertical as shown in Fig. 77, A, to resemble logs. Cut a door.

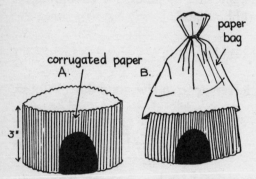

77. African native hut.

Cut the bottom from the brown bag, leaving a cylinder about 7 inches high. Bend the top of the corrugated cylinder inward and glue the bag to the base, permitting the bag to overhang the edge about an inch (B).

Squeeze in the top and hold with tape or string. Make several for games with wild animals and natives, or make a miniature size for an African diorama (p. 167).

Grocery-Carton Separators

Boxes sometimes contain corrugated separators to protect jars or bottles. These can be obtained free at drug or grocery stores if requested. Here are several uses:

1. Stand on one end for a doll cupboard. Paint if desired. If necessary, tape to the wall of the doll house to hold upright. If too large, cut *between* the separators (see dotted lines, Fig. 78) to prevent it falling apart.

2. Stand on one side to create an apartment house for

miniature dol s. Tape to a side of the carton it came in, or the box itself, to prevent falling.

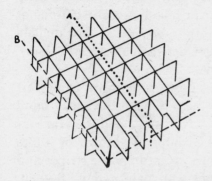

78. Grocery-carton separators.

3. Use as an aviary (home for birds) by turning on its side and following directions in (2). Make miniature birds following the patterns in Figs. 30 and 31. Attach birds to a string and tape the string to the top of each section for individual cages. Add this to a zoo.

4. Cut the depth of the separators in half along broken lines as shown (Fig. 79). This will create small pens for a zoo or stockyard, or low dividers for a hobby collection.

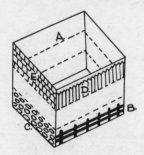

79. Corrals, fences and walls made from a grocery carton.

5. Cut on dotted lines, and then along broken lines, to fit a small box or drawer. Use as a separator for jewelry, combs, small toys, trinkets.

Corrals, Fences, Stone Walls

Cut with shears, or slice off with a heavy knife, 2-inch-deep, unbroken sections from a small grocery carton, as shown in Fig. 79, A. Use as corrals, zoo pens, yard or field fences or walls. For more realism, pencil in a design (below), and paint or color before cutting.

To make "logs," stroke up and down with brown paint, first a light stroke, then a dark. For railings, paint the background lightly if necessary to cover advertising, and the rails as shown (B). For a stone wall, paint gray, brown or white markings (C). For a picket fence, paint in white stripes and point at the top (D). For a brick wall, paint red, with white lines for bricks (E).

FRONTIER CRAFTS

Log Cabins

To make, use corrugated packing paper with the rough side out and running horizontally to resemble logs. Either a tiny one for a diorama (p. 167), or a shoe-box size for a town (p. 57) can be made the same way.

First, cut two rectangles, about 9 by 4 inches (Fig. 80, A). Cut two ends 6 inches wide by 4 inches high, but with a peaked top (B). Lay one on top of the other to match exactly. Cut a door along the dotted lines (A). Use a brass paper fastener for a handle. Use a craft razor (p. 8) to cut a window in one end piece.

Glue or plastic-tape the sides together. For the floor, cut a piece of carton 7 by 10 inches. Make lines on the plain side to resemble floor boards. Set up walls on floor and tape together around the inside.

Cut a roof 11 inches wide and 2 inches longer than distance around the triangular peak (B), to create eaves on both sides. Be sure the "logs" run across the paper, not lengthwise. Crease in the center for the ridge; glue into position. Use a light weight if necessary and allow a whole day to dry.

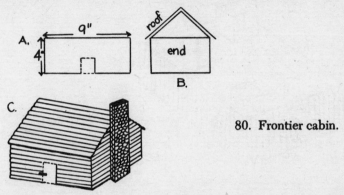

80. Frontier cabin.

For a chimney, cut two 7-by-1-inch strips and two 7-by-½-inch strips of gray or white cardboard. Draw lines as shown to resemble stones. Tape three sides together on the inside, tape the fourth side, and glue or plastic-tape to windowless end.

To use the cabin with miniature men, the back wall may be omitted, or just propped into position.

Experiment with matchstick or toothpick cabins, or twig-and-mud or rock-and-mud cabins. For these make the roof by covering a piece of cardboard with the "logs."

Fort

For miniature men, make a fort of corrugated wrapping paper. Cut four sides, as long as desired and 4 inches high. Be sure the corrugation runs up and down with the rough side out, to resemble logs, as shown in Fig. 81, A. If corrugated paper cannot be found, make walls of grocery carton sections cut tall enough for a fort (see "Corrals, Fences, Stone Walls." p. 90). Make a gate by cutting one side to one inch from the top and folding back. To hold closed when not in use, use brass paper fasteners as handles (on the *inside*), and wind thin string or a rubber band between the handles.

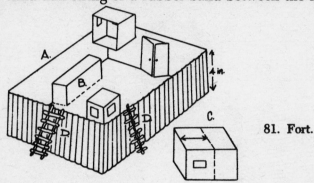

81. Fort.

For a shooting railing, glue or tape long, narrow boxes to the inner sides, cutting off on the dotted lines if too high (B). For corner blockhouses, cut small boxes (baby-shoe type) in half as shown (C). Be sure that the space marked by the arrow is about 2 inches higher than the fort walls. Cut windows in the box sides facing "the enemy." Glue or tape to opposite corners of the fort with the open side in. For scaling ladders, see below.

Ladders

For farm ladders, or fort-scaling ladders, cut pencil-thick twigs to the length desired. Nail together as shown in Fig. 81, D, or tie together with thongs (p. 114) or string.

Indian Palisade

The Eastern forest Indians, such as the Iroquois, built palisades (log fences for protection) around their village. To make one, use corrugated wrapping paper taped into a circle, or left open as shown (Fig. 82) to permit entry, with the "logs" running up and down. If wrapping paper is not available, follow directions for a log corral, p. 90, bending corners in to make it circular.

82. Indian palisade.

For "long houses," for inside the village, make long log cabins (p. 90). For tepees, see p. 112.

GENERAL CRAFT REFERENCES

Let's Make Paper Dolls, Vivian Huff, Harper, grades 1–3; *Rags, Rugs and Wool Pictures: First Book of Rug Hooking,* Ann Wiseman, Scribner's, grades 1–5. Grades 4–6: *Stitchery for Children,* Jacqueline Enthoven, Reinhold; *Knitting for Beginners* and *Crocheting for . . . ,* Jessie Rubenstone, Lippincott; *Fast and Easy Needlepoint,* Mary Anne Hodgson and Josephine Ruth Paine, Doubleday; *How to Paint with Water Colors: A Book for Beginners,* Arthur Zaidenberg, Vanguard; *Mobiles You Can Make,* Loretta Holz, Lothrop; *Simple Print-Making,* Peter Weiss, Lothrop; a series: *Look-and-Make Books: Exciting Things to Do with . . . (. . . Color,* Janet Allen; *. . . Nature Materials,* Judy Allen, etc.), Lippincott; *Christmas All Around the House: Traditional Decorations You Can Make,* Florence H. Pettit, Crowell; *Let's Make Presents,* Esther Hautzig, Crowell.

The Bibliography of Books for Children, Association for Childhood Education International, a serial, has excellent craft lists, such as sewing, cooking, colonial arts and crafts, Appalachian crafts, stitchery, rugmaking, knitting, nature, and ethnic crafts.

HOBBIES

While hobbies are special interests which give pleasure in spare time, they also have a real value for a young person. Some hobbies, such as history, science or nature, may lead to adult vocations. Others, such as art, music or stamp-collecting, may lead to lifetime enrichment. Hobbies provide a means of exploring the world.

There are various ways to add to the value of a hobby, but any of them become more fun when shared with another who has the same interest.

WAYS TO BUILD A HOBBY

Collecting

There are a number of special fields that can be *collected*: shells, rocks and other nature items, Indian, frontier or other handicrafts, coins, stamps, dolls and others.

A collection will be more interesting if kept together in a box or drawer. And it will mean more if it is *labeled*. When a rock is found and discovered to be quartz, it should be labeled before the name is forgotten (p. 160). And the collection will be most interesting of all if *mounted* or *sorted*.

SUGGESTED METHODS:
1. Plaster of Paris (p. 10).
2. In special boxes with separators—egg cartons, for ex-

ample. (To make a box, see "Grocery-Carton Separators," p. 88).

3. Glued to boards, or stiff cardboard such as the side of a grocery carton.

Scrapbook

This is particularly useful for building a hobby that can't be collected, such as outer space and the atom. A scrapbook can add to a collecting hobby by recording information found in magazines and newspapers, and notes from reading on the subject. It can include sketches made in the field, pictures from magazines, photographs.

A scrapbook can include also special crafts such as ink prints for leaves (p. 163), flowers, spatter prints (p. 164), designs.

Interest may be added to a scrapbook by including poetry on the subject chosen, and by arranging pictures and information artistically. Do not crowd too much on a page, and balance one large picture with several small.

The value of the scrapbook will be greatly increased if material is not pasted in until several pages are ready (unless it is loose-leaf), so that information on the same phase of the subject may be placed together. Keep materials in a file (p. 8) or envelope until ready.

Research

Build up a hobby interest through research. Read about the subject in library books, ask for a gift of one or two of the best for reference.

Make full use of the senses to *observe*—especially in the world of nature. Eyes trained to see the flitting of a bird in the bush, the dewy web of a spider in the early morn, will find not only more knowledge but more beauty.

And finally, an important part of research: experiment. Read, observe, and then, experiment. If a microscope is available, chip off a bit of rock to examine. Use a magnifying glass to study stamps. Compare the growth of a lima bean seed to a pea. Many hobbies offer a first-rate chance to see what makes the world work.

Craft Work

Another way to build a hobby is in the use of craft work. Model animals for an animal hobby in clay or papier-mâché, or carve them in soap. Sketch or paint birds for a bird collection, with a drawing of nest and egg beside each.

Even someone with little artistic ability can copy from books and magazines. A scrapbook on butterflies would profit from pictures drawn by looking at copies in books.

Related Activities

A last way to build a hobby is to do things related to the hobby. Travel will nearly always teach more about many hobbies, especially history, geography, nature, Indians. All areas, including your own, have museums and natural beauty spots and places of historic interest to investigate. Often there are musical records about a chosen subject, or movies, or special stores that deal in the materials needed.

This chapter has many suggestions for favorite hobbies. Several references are given for most of them, but a more complete list of fact books will be found on p. 2.

AIRPLANES AND JETS

Make a scrapbook of planes (p. 95). Build plastic models, which can be hung from mobiles in your room (p. 38). Visit airports and museums. Read some of the many books on the subject, both fact and fiction.

References

Wings: The Early Years of Aviation, Richard Rosenblum. Four Winds, grades 2–4; *How Airplanes Fly*, Walter Shepherd, Crowell, grades 4–7; *Fly It!*, John Kaufmann, Doubleday, making kites, gliders, etc., grades 4 up; *The First Book of Airplanes*, Jeanne Bendick, Watts, grades 3–5.

ART

Drawing, painting and sculpturing are not only wonderful hobbies in themselves; they also provide doors to other hobbies. If history is a special interest, study art from the drawings of primitive man to the present. If you are a nature lover, keep a sketch pad handy when outdoors, or a plastic bag of clay in your pocket, to sketch or mold what you see. If you find people absorbing, sketch their faces. Visit the art exhibits in museums, keep a scrapbook of magazine reproductions of great masterpieces. (See also "Perspective," p. 146.)

References

Newbery award winner: *The Many Ways of Seeing: An Introduction to the Pleasures of Art*, Janet Gaylord, Moore (World); *How to . . . (. . . Do Animals; . . . Faces*, etc.), Arthur Zaidenberg, Crowell, grades 3 up; *The Pantheon Story of American Art for Young People*, including American Indian, by Ariane (Ruskin) and Michael Batterberry, Pantheon, grades 5 up.

BRAIDING

Stitch or knot three strands of material together (Fig. 83, A.) Pin to a box, bedspread or other sturdy surface, to make the work go rapidly until a good start has been made.

First, pull the right strand (1) in front of the middle strand (2) as in B. Now pull the left strand (3) in front of the present middle strand (1), which was originally the right strand, as in C. This is the entire process of braiding: constantly pulling first the right strand, then the left strand, over the middle strand. Pull just tightly enough to make a neat, even braid.

When stopping work, loosely knot the ends of the strands to prevent unraveling until complete. When finished, stitch or knot strands together.

Braided Rug

Save all the bright, attractive socks that are to be discarded. Either nylon socks or cotton will do, but it is better not to mix them. Choose colors to suit the room for which the rug is

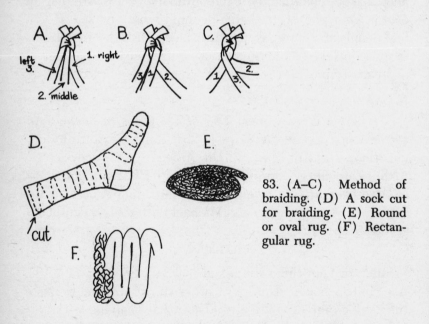

83. (A–C) Method of braiding. (D) A sock cut for braiding. (E) Round or oval rug. (F) Rectangular rug.

intended. Cut off the elastic band at the top. Begin cutting a long, winding strand that need not be broken until the toe is reached (Fig. 83, D). You will find the heel can be cut away entirely without breaking the strand. If the foot is stained or mended, the strand can end at the heel. It can then be kept as it is or cut into workable lengths if too long.

For a room rug, cut stocking strips ½-inch wide. For a doll rug, cut ¼-inch strips. In working, as the end of each strip of material is reached, stitch a new strand to the one in use.

To make the rug, braid several feet, then begin at the center for a round rug (E). Wind one row against the next, as shown, sewing firmly with a strong thread, braiding ahead several feet each time as you work. To avoid buckling do not sew too tight. Knot the sewing thread at frequent intervals to prevent unraveling in the wash.

For a rectangular rug, begin at one end (F).

CARS AND TRUCKS

Keep a scrapbook of the development of cars and trucks from an earlier day. Learn to recognize the various models on the road. Watch when an engine is being repaired and ask questions if permissible. Learn the purpose of each object on the dashboard. Buy and build the inexpensive plastic models, or make a toy car collection.

References

Model Cars and Trucks and How to Build Them and *Motors and Engines and How They Work,* both by Harvey Weiss, Crowell, grades 5 up; *Tin Lizzie,* by Peter Spier, Doubleday, grades 4–6, amusing fiction; *What Makes a Car Go?,* by Scott Corbett, Little, Brown, grades 3–6; *The First Book of Automobiles,* by Jeanne Bendick, Watts, grades 3–5; *The Trucks That Haul by Night,* by Leonard A. Stevens, Crowell, grades 1–3; *Truck Drivers: What Do They Do?,* by Carla Greene, Harper, grades 1–3; *Trucks,* by Gail Gibbons, Crowell, grades 3–7.

COINS

Begin by saving one new coin from each denomination: penny, nickel, dime, etc. Keep several of each for trading purposes, and replace worn coins with newer ones when possible, especially from rolls of new coins from the bank.

Ask older friends and relatives for coins now out of date. Ask traveling friends to bring back coins from other countries.

Keep each coin separately in flannel, small transparent plastic envelopes, or the plastic pages from a coin shop. These pages fit any standard 3-ring school binder. Separate the coins by countries, all Italian money together, all Canadian, and so on.

Coin books can help you understand and enjoy your collection.

References

Marvels of the Mint, by Oren Arnold, ancient coins to modern American, marks, etc., explained, grades 3–6; *Coins Have Tales to Tell,* by Frances Browin, American, anecdotes, Lippincott, grades 4 up; *Coin Collecting as a Hobby,* by Burton Hobson, Sterling, grades 5 up; *The Story of Coins,* by Sam Rosenfeld, Harvey House, grades 5 up.

COOKING

Cooking can be an absorbing hobby even to boys and men. Prepare very simple foods until you feel at home in the kitchen. Keep a card file of favorite recipes.

Here are a few ideas to begin on: popcorn, cinnamon toast, hot dogs, hamburgers, sugar cookies, gingerbread men; cooky-press cookies. A taffy pull is old-fashioned party fun.

(See also "Camping," p. 206, for camp cooking, and "Foods," p. 143.)

References

All, grades 4–7: *Kids Are Natural Cooks,* by Roz Ault, Houghton; *The Natural Snack Cook Book: 151 Good Things to Eat,* by Jill Pinkwater, Four Winds; *The Down to Earth Cookbook,* by Anita Borghese, Scribner's; *Many Hands Cooking: An International Cookbook for Girls and Boys,* by Terry Touff Cooper and Marilyn Ratner, Crowell, around the world, easy ingredients.

DOLLS

Many girls collect dolls, but few have a collection of *homemade* dolls. They can be made of clay, papier-mâché, or play dough; of beads, spools, yarn, foil, clothespins, nature items such as cones or shells. (See Index under "Dolls" for some suggestions. See also "Houses and Dolls," p. 55.)

References

Dolls, Dolls, Dolls, by Shirley Glubok, Follet, special photos, history, types, and houses from everywhere; *Make Your Own Dolls,* by Eleanor B. Heady, Lothrop; *Boxed-In Doll Houses,* by Betsy Pflug, Lippincott, using household items; *Dollhouse Magic: How to Make and Find Simple Dollhouse Furniture,* by P. K. Roche, Dial.

FLOWER ARRANGING

Study flower arrangements in books and magazines, and make a scrapbook of clever ideas. Visit flower displays at fairs and garden shows. Experiment with materials from your own yard.

Here are a few general rules on flower arrangement:

1. Use as few flowers as possible to permit each to stand out clearly.

2. Bouquets are most frequently in a triangular shape, narrow at top, extending out and down.

3. Put larger, heavier flowers near the base.

4. Have stems cut to various lengths. Pull off leaves below the water line to lengthen the life of the bouquet.

5. Pick colors that match, harmonize or contrast with the room. If the living room is pink, save the orange zinnias for the yellow kitchen.

Here are a few arrangements for beginners to try:

1. Use one, two or three flowers in a slim vase. Balance with leaves.

2. Float one, two or three flowers in a bowl, separated by floating leaves. This is especially good for flowers that do not last well otherwise, or those with stems that cannot be cut, such as camellias. Try roses, dahlias, gardenias.

3. Add a colorful rock or piece of deadwood or a small figurine to your arrangement. Or stand in front of a small screen (such as a thin bamboo mat stood on end). Or make or buy a wooden base to suit vase or bowl.

4. Collect and arrange attractively nature items such as dried seed pods, rocks, cones, moss, and so on. Use deadwood and driftwood. Experiment with gourds, dried corn, preserved leaves, nuts, etc. Place figurines nearby, such as pheasants.

Create small scenes—wood with animals, evergreens with cotton for snow, candle figures set in evergreen, etc.

GARDENING

Outdoor

Have the soil prepared in advance, and follow packet directions telling how deep and far apart to plant. Vegetables are fast-growing. Try radishes, onions, beets, lima beans, string beans, peas, tomatoes, corn.

The best flowers for children to grow are annuals, which

must be replanted every year but grow quite fast. Try zinnias, marigold, cosmos, and others suggested by a local store for showy beauty and rapid growth. Most annuals are planted in the spring. Flowers from seed are grown more easily if started in flats indoors (see below).

Bulbs also are easily grown. These can be "forced' 'indoors (see below), or planted deep outdoors in the autumn. Follow packet instructions for depth, place and time. These should not be planted in a row but grouped, three or four together, for bright spots of early color here and there in the garden. If planted at intervals throughout the fall the color will last longer.

Indoor

FORCING BULBS: For bright, long-lasting indoor color that requires no arranging, plant narcissus. Fill a pretty, low dish with water and sand, shells or gravel; place in it two or three bulbs. In a week start two or three more, and so on for continuous indoor bloom.

FORCING BRANCHES: Cut short branches from deciduous trees in late winter, place in water and await results. Fruit trees and pussy willows are especially rewarding.

SEED FLATS: Start flower seeds in small containers, to protect them from frost and give them a good start. If more than one type is planted, identify by writing name of plant on a popsicle stick and pushing it into the earth.

Half-gallon waxed milk cartons are excellent for flats. Remove one side. Fill about half full with topsoil, mixed with peat moss if available. Make two small furrows with a stick, and plant the seed about 1½ inches apart, following packet directions for depth. Keep the soil moist. When plants are

2 or 3 inches high and sturdy, transplant outdoors. Use a trowel and be careful to remove the surrounding soil with the plant to avoid shock to the roots. Have the new planting ground prepared ahead of time.

EXPERIMENTS: It is not necessary to dig up seeds outdoors to see how the garden is getting along. Instead, try the following:

1. Make a milk-carton "flat" (see above), and mark it off into fourteen small squares by laying string on the earth or drawing lines with a stick. The day you plant your seed outdoors, plant *one* of the same in the center of a corner square. Imbed a popsicle stick in the same square giving date. On the next day plant another of the same seeds in the next square, again labeling the day. (The day can be taped or scratched into the side of the box if preferred.) Then, each day for two weeks, plant one more seed. If the outdoor plants are not up by this time, mark off another milk carton and continue with one daily seed-planting until the outdoor plants are above an inch high.

When the outdoor plants are up, carefully uproot the milk-carton samples, working in order of the planting, to get a picture of the day-by-day development of seed-into-plant. Lima beans or peas are excellent for this experiment.

2. Plant a variety of seeds in milk-carton flats. These should be two inches apart. Try citrus seeds, date seeds, acorns, cotton, uncooked prunes. When walking pick up seeds in wild areas or along city parkways. Label each seed with the name, if possible, and date of planting. The date seeds at least can become beautiful indoor plants. Be sure to keep the soil damp.

3. For a short-term experiment, to watch seeds germinating from seed into plant, place fast-sprouting seeds such as

beans or peas in a glass jar. Have the jar lined with damp blotting paper curved inside, and drop the seeds between jar and liner. Keep blotting paper moist.

4. To prove that seeds reach for light and heat, plant a seed in a small box such as a whipping-cream carton. Plant in a corner opposite the pouring spout and fold half the spout down to make the hole smaller. If another box is used, cut a pen-sized hole away from the seed. The lid must be movable to permit watering, and the soil should be kept moist.

Watch the results, and you will discover that seeds, with no guiding eyes, always grow up toward the world instead of deeper into the soil.

5. Water plants: For a beautiful indoor vine, half-submerge a sweet potato in water and watch it sprout. If vine becomes stringy, pinch off gangly ends. Place a carrot half-submerged in water, after cutting all but the top one-half-inch of carrot plus one inch of greenery.

References

A Beginner's Book of Vegetable Gardening, Sigmund A. Lavine, Dodd, grades 5 up; *Newer and Better Organic Gardening,* Burke Davis, Putnam, grades 6–9; *Indoor Gardening,* D. X. Fenton, Watts, grades 4–7; *Kids Outdoor Gardening,* Aileen Paul, Doubleday, grades 4–6; *Flowers Are for Keeping: How to Dry Flowers and Make Gifts and Decorations,* Joella Cramblit and Jo Ann Loebell, Messner, grades 5 up; *A Flower with Love,* Bruno Munari, Crowell, flower arranging, grades 4 up.

GEOGRAPHY

One of the best ways to learn of places is to study maps. Whenever there is mention of a certain place on TV or in books or conversation, look it up in the atlas or on a globe.

Use wall-board panels (from lumberyards) to display a world map and one of the United States, perhaps in a hall.

Make a collection of maps. Keep a scrapbook (p. 95) of places of especial interest to you. Travel of course is ideal for a geography hobby, but reading is satisfying too. (See "Geography, p. 144.)

References

North, South, East, West, Franklin M. Branley, Harper, directions: up, down, left, right, around the world, grades 1–3. Grades 4–7: series: *Looking at . . . (. . . China,* Noel Gray; . . . *Israel,* Jonathon Rutland, etc.), Lippincott; *The Land and People of . . . (. . . England,* Alicia Street; . . . *Mexico,* Elsa Larraide), Harper. Also, *They Put Out to Sea,* Roger Duvoisin, Knopf, the map and how it grew; *Atlas of World Wildlife,* Rand McNally, all ages.

HISTORY, ARCHEOLOGY AND ANTHROPOLOGY

History, the story of man's past, and biography, the stories of the men who made that history, form an interesting hobby. Add archeology, the study of the cities and objects earlier civilizations have left behind, to broaden an understanding of the past, and anthropology, the study of mankind.

There is a world of books in these fields. There are colorful magazine advertisements telling one special story, suitable for a scrapbook collection (p. 95). There are museums and historical places to visit wherever you travel.

Read historical fiction and then look up the background in the encyclopedia. In this field try the Joseph Altsheler books on the French and Indian, Texas and Civil wars and the many books on pioneers, Colonial days, Indians. Read biographies of the great scientists, discoverers, and leaders in thought, government and art.

References

By Joan Fritz: *And Then What Happened, Paul Revere?*, *Who's That Stepping on Plymouth Rock?*, etc., Coward, grades 3–5. *Mysteries from the Past,* Thomas Aylesworth, ed., Doubleday, archeological puzzles, grades 5 up; *The Caves of the Great Hunters,* Hans Baumann, Pantheon, cavemen, France, grades 5 up; *Maria's Cave,* William H. Hooks, Coward, cavemen, Spain, grades 3–7. See also Prehistoric Times, p. 116.

HOME DECORATING

Make a scrapbook of magazine pictures showing rooms that attract you. Learn to observe unusual homes you visit, and note professional decorating tricks in model houses. Try to discover the reasons for their appeal.

Home Decorating Ideas

1. Pictures and wall ornaments should be at eye level. Small items seem more important in pairs or grouped.
2. Choose three or four colors for a room and try to hold to these. You might choose pink and green, for example, with touches of gray and white. Experiment with a doll house and furniture (p. 65).
3. Balance figured surfaces with plain. Too many designs are confusing to the eye.
4. Avoid clutter. Dressers, tables, headboards should be bare except for a very few decorative items. Change these to add interest and prevent tiring of your treasures. If no table runner is used, glue bits of felt or Styrofoam to the bottoms of vases, jewel boxes, etc., to protect furniture.
5. Suit the decoration to the room: woodsy arrangements in rustic rooms; shells in rooms with a tropical motif or in the bath, adding fish net, baskets, ceramic mermaids, and fish, etc. (For additional decorating ideas, see pp. 29–47.)

INDIAN LORE

Indians lived the wild, free life most young people would like to live. Reading about their lives and legends and making their crafts provides a satisfying hobby. There are many books, both fiction and fact, based on their lives. Many museums throughout the country have Indian displays to visit when traveling.

References

Series: *American Indian Tribes*, Sonia Bleeker, Morrow, "still tops," grades 4–6; *The Art of . . . (. . . The Plains Indians; . . . The Woodland Indians*, etc.), Shirley Glubok, Macmillan, grades 3 up. *Talking Bones: Secrets of Indian Mound Builders*, William O. Steele, Harper, grades 2–5. Grades 4–7: *The Book of Indian Crafts and Indian Lore*, Julian H. Saloman, Harper; *Let's Be Indians*, Peggy Parish, Harper; *The Sound of Flutes and. Other Indian Legends*, Richard Erdoes, ed., Pantheon; *Many Winters: Prose and Poetry of the Pueblos*, Nancy Wood, Doubleday; grades 6 up: *Oldest Man in America*, Ruth Kirk with Richard D. Daugherty, Morrow; *Many Smokes, Many Moons: A Chronology of American Indian History Through Indian Art*, Lippincott.

Indian Designs

Designs for decorating tepees, costumes, etc., were often geometric figures: circles, squares, triangles, representing the world they knew—mountains, rain, thunder, and so on. A number of these designs are shown (Fig. 84, A). Use graph paper to create your own. In most patterns, an uneven number of beads or squares is used, to permit centering.

Indian Symbols

These were used for messages and decorations, to tell a story (Fig. 84, B).

Indian Scout Pictographs

These were rather generally used symbols (Fig. 84, C).

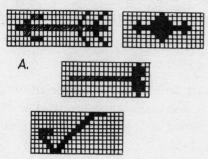

A.

B.

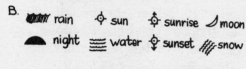

🐛 rain ♢ sun ♢ sunrise ☽ moon

night ≋ water ♀ sunset ⫽ snow

84. (A) Indian designs. (B) Symbols for picture writing. (C) Scout pictographs.

C.

camp big town of to tall timber

six days of peace tracks on trail

Trail Signs

Indians developed several methods of leaving messages on the trail for sharp-eyed followers to read. They were copied by the pioneers and trappers. The most secret was tree blazing, when trees would be marked in a certain manner to serve as a map for those following. This should not be done today

this is the trail   turn right   turn left   warning

this is the trail   turn right   turn left   warning

85. Trail signs: rocks, grass.

on public trails, but the piling of rocks or twisting of grasses in special ways to tell a message harm nothing and give practice in scouting (Fig. 85).

"Warning" (shown) means a change that might be missed, a danger ahead, or other unusual object or event.

Indian Crafts

The following Indian craft articles can be made in miniature for a hobby collection or use in dioramas (p. 167) or bark scenes (p. 170). Use also as room decorations, party invitations or favors, or for trinket gifts.*

Materials such as feathers, beads, and leather can be purchased at hobby shops (get scrap leather), or specialty shops for Indian goods or leather. In many cases home supplies can be substituted, such as cardboard or felt for leather, paper feathers for real feathers, homemade beads (p. 28).

TOTEM POLES: These were used by the Far Northwest Indians to tell a family or tribal story.

1. Choose five nuts. Shown in Fig. 86, A, are two walnuts, three hazel nuts. Paint faces on each nut.

On a 2-by-4-inch piece of wood, glue half of a nutshell, flat side down. To this glue one of the nut faces. When thoroughly dry, glue another on top, and so on until the "totem" is in position. Glue a tiny feather or feather tip to the top nut. To one side glue a little beaver. The one shown is made of a pecan body, hazelnut face, toothpick legs and leather tail. All pieces were glued except the legs, which were pushed into holes pricked ahead of time.

2. Poster-paint an empty bathroom-tissue roll. Decorate as desired. The one shown (Fig. 86, B) is painted yellow with

* Many of the Indian objects described were created by members of the Pawnee Tribe, Wanona Nation, Y-Indian Guides of Van Nuys, Calif.

cardboard wings, one red, one green, inserted into slits in the side. The beak is a small piece of black paper folded lengthwise and bent down at the end, inserted into a triangular slit. The eyes are brass paper fasteners; the feathers, blue craft paper; the claws, black paint.

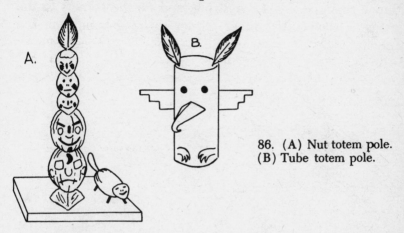

86. (A) Nut totem pole.
(B) Tube totem pole.

Several of these, each with a different design, can be glued or taped together and held firm by small sticks taped to the inside.

3. Spool totem pole: For a base, use a 4-inch square of plywood, or glue four thicknesses of cardboard together tightly. Paint. Paint three to five large spools, as many as the number of totem faces desired. Plan each totem on paper for best results. Use felt, cotton, rickrack, small feathers, paper, sequins, beads, etc., for decoration or design.

When dry, glue one on top of the other.

TRAVOIS: A travois (trav-wah) was used by the Plains Indians as a carry-all when camp was broken. Shafts were tied to the ponies, or sometimes dogs (among the Eastern Forest Indians), dragging on the ground behind, and to these were strapped rolls containing all the tribal belongings (Fig. 87, A).

To make a small travois, cut two 6-inch twigs and a strip of leather or tan cloth 3 inches long. One end should be one inch wide, the other 1½ inches. Punch holes in each corner, cut 3-inch thongs (p. 114) or string, and tie the corners to the twigs as shown. Use other thongs to tie a bundle on the travois.

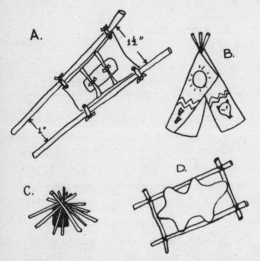

87. Indian crafts. (A) Travois. (B) Tepee. (C) Campfire. (D) Drying skin.

In addition to the uses suggested under "Indian Crafts," above, this travois is suited for play, with miniature men and horses.

TEPEE: To make a tepee for use in dioramas (p. 167) or bark scenes (p. 170), cut a piece of tan craft paper 6 by 2½ inches. For an Indian village to use with miniature men, cut the paper approximately 6 by 12 inches.

Twist in the fingers until shaped as shown in Fig. 87, B. Round off the bottom with a scissors, to stand level, and cut the end of the paper to create the desired shape. Before gluing, open out and decorate with Indian designs or signs (p. 108). Glue ends together, one over the other. When dry, cut a triangular opening as shown. For greater realism, glue or tape twigs inside the top hole.

CAMPFIRE: This can be any size desired. To create a miniature "fire" for a bark scene, diorama or shadow box, cut twelve thin twigs each one inch long. Cut a ½-inch length of much thicker twig and paint red with nail enamel, to resemble a log on fire. Glue this to a base. Around it, tepeewise, glue the small twigs (Fig. 87, C).

DRYING SKIN: Cut a piece of preferably thin leather about 3½ by 2½ inches, or any size desired. Shape this like a drying animal skin, with legs, head and tail, as shown (Fig. 87, D).

Choose two 4½-inch twigs, two 3-inch twigs, and tie together with thong (p. 114) or heavy dark string, as shown, for a rack. Glue the "skin" to this.

This can be pinned to the wall of a log cabin (p. 90) or hung between trees for a bark scene or diorama.

KNOT TYING

The ring hitch is one of the most practical knots. Use it to fasten items to a belt, leaving the hands free, or for mooring boats, or for yarn fringe:

Use a double rope, as shown (88, A), or a single rope or string doubled back. The center loop in this case (B) is

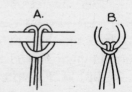

88. Ring hitch, a knot of many uses.

pulled up from behind the belt, yarn hole or other object.
The loop is held open while the ends are pulled through it
from the front, then closed by pulling end taut.

References

Girl Scout and Boy Scout handbooks, the encyclopedia, and
manuals at ship supply stores.

LEATHERWORK

In the yellow pages of the phone book are listings of
leather or hobby shops that sell inexpensive scrap leather.
Leatherwork also requires lacing, and a leather punch. The
cheapest type of punch resembles a pencil with a hole where
the point should be. Pound on a board to prevent dulling.

Always draw a pattern for leatherwork first on paper and
use this for a guide.

Leather Thongs

Many crafts call for leather thongs for lacing or tying, but
the straight edges of the scrap leather, which have so many
uses, need not be wasted on these. Use any odd shape, cutting continuously around the edge in a thin strip until the
necessary length is reached.

References

Leatherwork, Sylvia Grainger, Lippincott, grades 6 up.

Reference

PEN PALS

To find a pen pal to correspond with from another section
of the country or the world, write: International Friendship
League, 22 Battery March, Boston, Mass. 02109. To write to
someone in a foreign country, state your name and address,

your age, your interests, and the country with which you wish to correspond. For pen pals in this country, look for addresses in children's magazines, such as *Junior Natural History*, American Museum of Natural History, Central Park West at 79th St., New York. Libraries often carry such magazines.

PETS

Animal lovers will find pets an interesting hobby if permissible. Make a scrapbook (p. 95) of pets and information concerning them. Read books about animals. (See also "Wild Pets," p. 166.)

References

Pets, Frances N. Chrystie, Little, Brown, care and training, all ages; *Your First Pet and How to Take Care of It*, Carla Stevens, Macmillan, grades 2–4; *A Great Aquarium Book: The Putting-It-Together Guide for Beginners*, Jane Sarnoff, Scribner's; *Pets and More Pets*, ten tales, Crowell, grades 4–6; *Animal Doctors: What Do They Do?*, Carla Greene, Harper, grades 1–3; *Animal Hospital*, Melvin Berger, Crowell, grades 4–7; *Old Yeller*, Fred Gipson, Harper, grades 5 up; *The Incredible Journey*, Sheila Burnford, Little, Brown, grades 4–6; *Animal Babies*, Arthur Gregor, Harper, grades 1–3; *A Fish Hatches*, Joanna Cole, Morrow, grades 1–3.

Most pet stores have booklets on the care of specific animals. For other pets, see also: Aquarium, p. 155; Birds, p. 155; Insects, p. 159; Wild Pets, p. 166. For general interest, see Animals, pp. 155 and 210. Also, send for *Hobby Publications*, Superintendent of Documents, U.S. Government Printing Office, Washington, D.C. (free).

PHOTOGRAPHY

This is an expensive hobby, so begin with a small, cheap camera. It is wise to make a case or shoulder bag for it, or at least to wear it on a string around the neck when on a trip. Also attach a band of adhesive tape to camera carrying name, address and telephone number.

Study each group of pictures to see what is wrong. If information is sent by the developing company, read it carefully. It is cheaper and more fun to learn to develop prints at home.

Keep pictures together in an album. Even a loose-leaf notebook will do if necessary, with five-and-ten photo tabs used to hold the pictures and permit later removal. File them (p. 8) until ready to arrange in an album. Label lightly on the back with names, dates, and places. Transfer this information to a strip of white paper to be glued beneath the picture, or write it under the picture in white ink.

References

The Complete Beginner's Guide to Photography, George Laycock, Doubleday, grades 5 up; *How to Photograph Your World,* Viki Holland, Scribner's, the composition and planning behind a picture, grades 4–6; *The Story of American Photography,* Martin W. Sandler, Little, Brown, grades 6 up.

PREHISTORIC TIMES

Build a collection of five-and-ten prehistoric monsters and cave people, for use in games. Use them to build dioramas (p. 167) in a grocery carton, or for a home museum display. Visit museums for prehistoric displays.

References

Grades 1–3: *Dinosaur Time,* Peggy Parish, Harper; *Fossils Tell of Long Ago; My Visit to the Dinosaurs; Digging up Dinosaurs and Early Birds,* John Kaufmann, Crowell. Grades 3–5: *They Lived with the Dinosaurs,* Russell Freedman, Holiday House, other animals. Grades 4–7: *How Did We Find Out About Our Human Roots?,* Isaac Asimov, Walker; *Dinosaurs of North America,* Helen Roney Sattler, Lothrop; *People of the Ice Age,* Ruth Goode, Crowell, man's seven gifts; *Prehistoric America,* Anne Terry White, Random House.

SEWING

Sewing can be the most useful of hobbies. Following are simple beginner items.

See, grades 4 up: *I Love to Sew,* Barbara Corrigan, Doubleday; *It's Easy to Sew with Scraps and Remnants,* Carol Inouye, Doubleday; *Sock Craft: Toys, Gifts and Other Things to Make,* Helen Roney Sattler, Lothrop; *Plenty of Patches: . . . Patchwork, Quilting, Appliqué,* Marilyn Ratner, Crowell; *Fun with Crewell Embroidery,* Erica Wilson, Scribner's; *Braid Craft,* Donna M. Lightbody, Lothrop.

Felt Belt

Cut a 2-inch strip of felt, one inch shorter in length than your waist. On the last 2 inches on each end, stitch a piece of thin leather or heavy material underneath to strengthen the felt. The thread should match the felt. On each end punch or cut three ⅛-inch holes in a row (Fig. 89). Use leather thong

89. Felt belt.

(p. 114) or ribbon to lace through the holes for a tie. Decorate the felt by gluing to it tiny bits of contrasting colors of felt cut in geometric figures, toy shapes, or dolls. Or stitch sequins or beads from a notion counter to the belt in a pattern.

Dress Tie

Buy one yard of one-inch-wide satin or grosgrain ribbon in a pretty pattern and color. Knot loosely around the neck

to measure for length, and cut if necessary. Neatly hand-
stitch the two ends to prevent fraying, and then decorate
with sequins or beads, using initials, circles, lines, etc. Learn
to tie a four-in-hand (man's tie) knot. Wear with blouses or
give as a gift (Fig. 90).

90. Dress tie.

Elf Bag

This requires a 12-by-13-inch piece of felt. For a girl's
purse cut a 12-inch square of felt leaving a thin strip along
the side; make a 6-inch square for a doll's, with all other
measurements half-size too.

Fold the 12-inch square as shown (Fig. 91, A), stitching the
numbered seams together 3½ inches toward the center, (1)

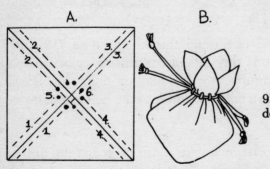

91. Elf bag for girl or
doll.

to (1), (2) to (2), and so on. Turn the other side out, and sew on curtain rings or felt strips as shown by the dots (A). This is the basic purse.

Now use the leftover strip to cut two handles, each 12 by ½ inch. Loop one through each ring, beginning and ending at (5), tying tightly and then fringing the handle edge beyond the knot. Now loop the second handle, beginning and ending at (6). Pull up cords and the elf bag is done (B).

Pillows

Cut a 13-inch square basic pillow case from an unworn section of old sheeting, unbleached muslin, etc., folded double. Turn wrong side out and machine-stitch three sides. Turn right side out and fill with feathers or kapok. Turn the edges of the fourth side in and machine-stitch.

For a round pillow, cut two circles 13 inches across, using a plate for a pattern if you have no pencil compass. Stitch together, leaving about one-third open for filling.

The pillow cover is made in the same manner except that it is 14 inches across, and the fourth side is hand-stitched for removal of the cover for washing.

To decorate:

1. Quilt a cover (see p. 120).

2. Draw simple designs or get them from other sources (Fig. 92, A), tracing them to a 14-inch square or circle of bleached muslin or other solid-color or white material. Outline the designs in a simple embroidery stitch (p. 121) in colors to suit the room.

3. Ask friends to write their names, in pencil and rather large writing, on the pillow-cover material. Embroider each in a different color, or all in one color (B).

4. Combine quilt and embroidery patterns by making every other square plain white, with a design or a signature

embroidered on the white. The alternate squares will be of
various materials (C).

5. Make a pillow cover of the curtain material of the room.
The plainer pillows, such as the signature case, can be
brightened with an edging of washable and prewashed curtain fringe, with a row of quilting or with rickrack, or with
yarn tassels (p. 77) tied to the corners.

92. Pillows to make. (A)
Embroidered designs. (B)
Signature pillow. (C)
Combined quilting and
embroidery. (D) All-over
quilted pattern.

Quilting

Piecing a quilt is the process of cutting leftover scraps of
new cloth into shapes, and stitching these together in a
pattern, to form a whole cloth.

To quilt some pillows for a room, first make the basic
pillow (p. 119). Cut several pretty, washable materials into
shapes that will fit well together, such as triangles, diamonds,
squares, long bars.

Lay the patterns out in a pleasing combination. Patterned areas are more attractive when separated by plain (Fig. 92, D). Stitch pieces together, making the quilted front one inch larger all around than the basic pillow will be. Stitch three edges, wrong side out, to a back of sheeting or bleached muslin; turn right side out, put basic pillow inside and hem the fourth edge by hand to permit removal for washing.

Sewing Stitches

The sewing stitches pictured in Fig. 93 are the most basic stitches used: blanket stitch (A), basting stitch (B), button-

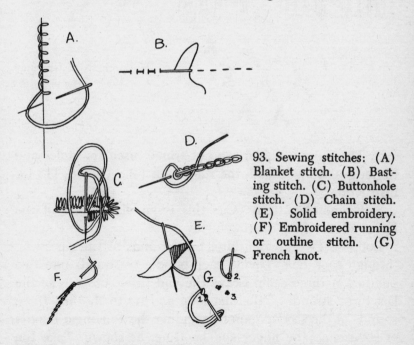

93. Sewing stitches: (A) Blanket stitch. (B) Basting stitch. (C) Buttonhole stitch. (D) Chain stitch. (E) Solid embroidery. (F) Embroidered running or outline stitch. (G) French knot.

hole stitch (C), chain stitch (D), solid embroidery (E), embroidered running or outline stitch (F), French knot (G).

To make a French knot, wind thread around needle three times (1), push needle into cloth (2) and pull thread through for finished knot (3).

How to Fringe

1. On material that doesn't unravel, fringe can be made by cutting at intervals the entire distance, as with Indian costumes (Fig. 94, A). Other types of fringe:

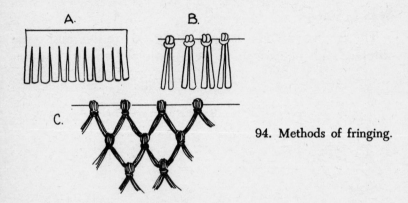

94. Methods of fringing.

2. The most common type of fringe, used for stoles and rug edges, is made with the ring hitch (B). (See p. 113 for instructions.)

3. Diamond pattern (C): this is an elaboration of the fringe above, using the ring hitch.

Loop-tie (with a ring hitch) six strands of yarn or string through each hole. Divide each bundle of strands into two bundles of three each. Leave the end three loose. Take the last three strands of the first loop and tie to the first three strands of the second loop by winding the combined bundle of six around the finger and knotting, as shown. Take the second three strands of the second loop and the first three strands of the third and knot, and so on across the row.

A second row of ties, to form the diamond, is made in the same manner as shown.

4. Pull fringe: use for card-table or doll-table covers, napkins, runners. This is easiest with materials that unravel easily and have a rather coarse weave.

Remove all selvage. Loosen with pin or fingernail the last thread of the cut edge of material. Pull gently until it comes away from the material. Continue, thread by thread, until the desired amount of fringe has been created.

If materials with this fringe are shaken while damp, they can be ironed more easily. Gently run a clean comb through to straighten knotted fringe.

Laundry-Bag Doll

Cut two circles 18 inches in diameter of checked gingham or other material. Cut a slit in one, to the center of the circle, hemming each side (Fig. 95, A). Stitch circles together,

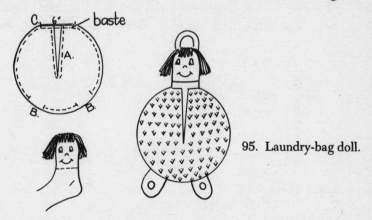

95. Laundry-bag doll.

inside out, leaving two 3-inch openings at the bottom (B), and a 6-inch opening at the top. When right side out, insert two flaps of white felt, or other washable material in bottom openings and stitch tight for doll's shoes (see finished bag, Fig. 94). Turn the 6-inch opening under and hem (C). Also run a heavy basting thread around this opening.

Use the toe of a new, white, man's work sock for a head. Stuff the toe with old nylon stocking strips and hem just ahead of the heel. Create a face with embroidery thread or buttons. Add yarn hair. To the top of the head attach firmly a loop of doubled material stitched together, for a handle to hang on a closet wall.

Now insert the head in the 6-inch opening, draw the basting thread tight and stitch the "body" to the head very firmly, before removing bastings.

Stuff the doll with soiled hose or other small laundry items by inserting in the front slit.

Travel Shoe Bags

Lay a man's shoe on two thicknesses of cloth. Mark a rectangle two inches larger than the shoe all the way around, and cut. Machine-stitch around three sides, leaving two

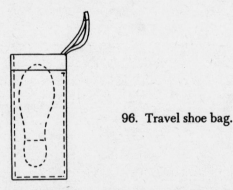

96. Travel shoe bag.

inches of the last side unstitched as shown (Fig. 96). Fold the open end down one inch and hem. Be sure to leave open one end of the hem. Through this run a tie from old pajamas, or mending tape. Stitch ends of tie together to prevent slipping out.

Make two of these for each pair of shoes. Use in suitcases to prevent shoes from soiling clothes. Shoe bags make excellent gifts.

SHIPS

Build or buy small models in bottles, etc. Build plastic models of famous ships. Make a scrapbook of pictures and news stories about them. Boys may find a Sea Scout troop near their home.

Read stories of the sea, the Navy, and pirates. When visiting harbor towns, investigate chances to board Navy ships, fishing boats, or historic ships such as *Old Ironsides* or the *Balclutha*, a sailing merchant ship in San Francisco Harbor.

References

Grades 4–7: *Ship Models and How to Build Them*, Harvey Weiss, Crowell; *Oars, Sail and Steam*, Edwin Tunis, Crowell; *Blow Ye Winds Westerly: The Seaports and Sailing Ships of Old New England*, Crowell; *Thor Heyerdahl and the Reed Boat "Ra,"* Barbara Beasley Murphy and Norman Baker, Lippincott; *By Wagon and Flatboat*, Enid La Monte Meadowcroft, Crowell. *Up and Down the River: Boat Poems,* Claudia Lewis, Harper, grades 1–3.

STAMPS

Stamp collecting can be the most expensive of hobbies, but a fine collection that will give much pleasure can be built up with very little cost.

Some collectors save cancellations and postmarks as well and cut out the entire corner. Some soak stamps from letters. Some save only new stamps, in units of four. An amateur can suit himself, but it is wise to save several of each for trading purposes.

Remove stamps from old envelopes. Check the post office regularly for new issues.

Keep stamps sorted by country and boxed until ready to mount them. Albums can be purchased for this purpose, but beginners usually have more fun using plain white paper in a loose-leaf book, mounting the stamps with stamp hinges or plastic protectors. This permits later removal without damage if desired. Keep all of one country together. With American stamps, sort by denomination: threes, fours, and so on. As the collection grows, you may wish to place all Great Men together, or all state commemoratives; all sports or toys, or flowers or animals, etc.

References

A *Child's World of Stamps: . . . Fun and Facts . . .* , Mildred DePree, *Parents; Beginning Stamp Collecting*, Bill Olcheska, Walck.

TRAINS

Build up a toy train collection. Make plastic or cardboard models of real trains. Visit locomotive collections or museums when possible, especially when traveling.

Learn the railroad songs, or collect records: "My Father Was a Railroad Man," "I've Been Working on the Railroad," "Casey Jones," etc.

References

Grades 3–6: *Railroads*, T. Harvey, Lerner; *End o' Steel*, Glen Dines, Macmillan, building the transcontinental railroads; *Trains Around the World*, Octopus Books. Grades 5–8: Harvey Weiss, Crowell: *How to Run a Railroad*, about model trains; *Model Buildings and How to Make Them,* good for model railroads; *Supertrains,* John Gabriel Navarra, Doubleday; *Railroad Yard,* Paul C. Ditzel, Messner; *Color Treasury of Model Trains,* Crescent; *Railroads in the Days of Steam,* Albert L. McCready, Harper, the first American railroad, railroads in the Civil War, etc.

UNITED STATES

Make several expandable scrapbooks with two pages for each state. Check the local library or the encyclopedia under state names, and sketch state flowers, trees, birds and other symbols. Add pictures of famous places, great events or great men from each. List important facts. (This can also be done for one state.)

References: Courage to Adventure, Child Study Association of America, Crowell, bicentennial anthology of American children in our 200 years, grades 4–6. See also p. 209.

WEAVING

The principles of weaving, given below, may be adapted to many other objects, such as doll rugs, or wall "tapestries" for doll houses.

Round Purse

Cut two disks of heavy cardboard 6 or 8 inches in diameter, depending on the size purse you wish. Use a pencil compass or small plate bottom for a pattern. With a ruler and pencil, mark each disk in halves, then quarters, etc., until there are sixteen lines. Readjust three or four of them as shown (Fig. 97, A) to make room for a seventeenth line, and notch edges about ¼ inch deep as shown. Each disk forms a loom for half the purse.

Paste the end of a piece of yarn over the center of the
loom. When dry, start at the center and wind the yarn out
to a notch (B-1), behind the loom to another notch (2),
back to the center (3), on across to (4-5-6), and so on until
the yarn has been pulled through each notch, ending in the
center. The last strand from notch to center will be double,
but is handled as if it were single.

Now you have your warp. Fasten the weaving yarn (woof)
to the center, run the end through a large blunt needle (a

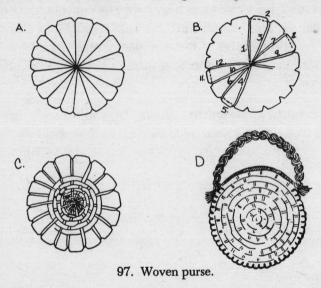

97. Woven purse.

real yarn needle is best), and begin to weave in and out (C).
The strands you weave *under* the first time will be woven
over the next time, reversing with each row.

When one strand of yarn is finished, tie a new one onto it
with a tight knot, cutting ends close. Different colors can be
woven in if desired.

When first disk is filled in, remove from loom by slipping
loops off the notches. When the second circle is woven, turn

them wrong side out, hold together and overcast or blanket-stitch (p. 121) together, leaving the top third free. This can be fastened with snaps, or the purse can be lined and a zipper added.

For a handle, knot together six 14-inch strands of yarn. Make two more similar bundles, and braid these together (p. 97). Knot on both ends and fasten across the side of the purse, or fasten on one side only, to dangle (D).

Woven Belt

To make a belt (Fig. 98), follow the pattern for the purse above. Make the loom 2 inches in diameter. Use yarn or raffia, and make four disks. Stitch to a five-and-ten belt, or a felt belt (p. 117). Buckle belt in back.

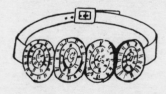

98. Woven belt.

References: Yarn: *Things It Makes and How to Make Them,* J. Perrott, C. Meyer, Harcourt; *Fun with Weaving,* A. Gilbreath, Morrow.

WHITTLING

Woodcarving is a very old and very appealing hobby, and an easy one, say those who practice it. The main needs are soft wood (balsa, pine, cottonwood), and a very sharp knife. No irresponsible person should take up this hobby. Whittling is for the careful.

References: Grades 5 up: Harvey Weiss: *How to Carve Wood and Stone,* Addison-Wesley, *Hammer & Saw, . . . Woodworking for Kids,* Frank D. Torre, Doubleday.

WRITING

Writing a Story

It is sometimes hard to get started in writing a story. Often a picture in a magazine or book will seem to have a story behind it. Pick up a rock, or a penny, and write its tale. Observe a stranger closely, in a market or elsewhere, when he or she is not aware of it, and make up a story about him. Write a story or play with animals or toys as characters.

Picture Story

Write a story, but use a picture instead of a word whenever possible. Adjectives and nouns often can be replaced with pictures, such as a tree for the word "tree." For "She was so happy," the word "happy" could be replaced with a tiny round face with a smile.

Writer's Motto

An old saying, given as advice by writers to those who wish to write, is this: "Attach the seat of the pants to the seat of the chair—and write." In other words, don't just *think* writing would be fun, but do it.

WRITING AND CULTURAL REFERENCES

Grades 1–3: *Signs and Symbols Around the World*, Elizabeth Helfman, Lothrop. Grades 4–7: *Turn Not Pale, Beloved Snail*, Jacqueline Jackson, Little, Brown; *In Your Own Words*, Sylvia Cassedy, Doubleday; *Communication: From Stone Age to Space Age*, Harry Edward Neal, Messner; *The Beginning of Words: How English Grew*, Colin Pickles and Lawrence Meynell, Putnam; *The First Book of Words: Their Family History*, Sam and Beryl Epstein, Watts; *All About Language*, Mario Pei, Lippincott, evolution of language into branches, emphasis on English; *How Art and Music Speak to Us*, Cornelia Spencer, Crowell, music, dance, painting, sculpture, from the cave to the present; *Favorite Poems Old and New*, selected by Helen Ferris, Doubleday.

FUN WITH SCIENCE

Over twenty-five centuries ago men were beginning to realize that the physical world was governed by unchanging laws. Thus scientists of every type have been studying, experimenting with and observing these laws for a long time. Each generation's men of science have built on the knowledge written down for them by earlier students.

This chapter delves into ten different fields of this vast store of knowledge.

HOW TO BE A SCIENTIST

1. Think your project through. Planning ahead saves time and money.

2. Read widely.

3. Question others. Talk with teachers, parents, other adults and school friends interested in the same field.

4. Work carefully as you go.

5. Do not be foolhardy. Dangerous materials should not be used by a young scientist except under supervision of an *informed* adult.

6. Observe carefully. Learn to *see* the world about you.

ASTRONOMY

Astronomy is the study of the heavens: the constellations, which are groups of stars that have seemed to form a picture to all men everywhere since the dawn of history; the planets, which are satellites circling our most important star, the sun;

and the stars themselves, the glowing heavenly bodies from which the planets receive reflected light.

The planets and stars are not so difficult to learn if the memory tricks given in many books are mastered first. The end stars of the most famous constellation, the Big Dipper, for example, point to the North Star—which is the last star in the handle of the Little Dipper. The Big Dipper's curving handle points directly to Arcturus—and that is a big reddish-orange beauty, the major star in the constellation Boötes (The Herdsman). These are just a few of many memory tricks.

The locations of the constellations at the four seasons may be found in a number of books, kits or charts (see below). Such reference materials also show individual constellations with drawings picturing how they appeared to the Greeks who named them so long ago (for American Indian names, see p. 134).

A moonless night is best for observation. With book or chart and a flashlight, locate the constellations. Then make "stargazers" (below) so that you will know your favorite constellations without referring to a book.

Astronomy Experiments

To understand day and night, imagine a flashlight is the sun and a ball the earth. Darken the room and flash the light on the ball. Turn the ball slowly from west (left) to east (right). This demonstrates how there can be dawn, daylight, twilight and night in different parts of the world at the same time.

TELESCOPE: At an optometry store, buy two lens holders and two inexpensive lenses: one thin convex lens, one thick convex lens.

Place lenses in lens holders. Turn a yardstick edge up, or

use a dowel stick, and firmly wire the thin lens about one inch from one end of the stick. Wire the thick lens one inch from the other end, but loosely enough to move back and forth slightly (Fig. 99).

99. Telescope

Use this telescope to make objects, including the moon, seem larger and closer. Look from the thick-lens edge, adjusting this lens as necessary.

STARGAZERS: 1. Save cardboard tubes from paper towels, bathroom tissue, or foil. Stand a tube on black paper and cut

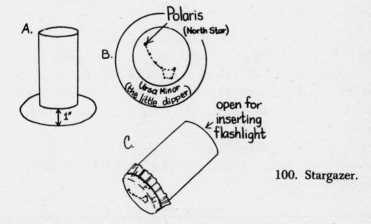

100. Stargazer.

a circle one inch larger all around, marking with a pencil the rim of the tube on the larger circle (Fig. 100, A).

Within the tube mark, draw a constellation, following a

pattern from a book. Make a hole for each star using a common pin. Prick smaller holes for the dimmer stars (B). Tie or tape the black circle to the end of the tube, or hold with a rubber band (C). Label the name of the constellation on the side. Use other tubes for other constellations. The tubes may be painted if desired.

As a group activity, each person can make a different constellation. When you know the constellations fairly well, cover the names and see how many you can identify.

The easiest way to observe through a "stargazer" is to go into a darkened room with a flashlight. Flash the light into the tube and aim it at the ceiling, where spots of light, shining through the pinpricks, will represent the constellation.

2. Use an oatmeal box or salt box. Remove the lid or one end. In the other punch out a diagram of a constellation. This will be more accurate if drawn on the box first to avoid errors in punching. Use as described under (1) above.

References

By Franklin Mansfield Branley: *The Sky Is Full of Stars,* Crowell, picture book introduction to stargazing, cartoon drawings, grades 1–3; *A Book of Planet Earth for You; A Book of the Milky Way Galaxy for You;* and *A Book of Stars for You,* grades 2–5; *Find the Constellations,* by H. A. Rey, Houghton, grades 3–6; *The Stars: Decoding Their Message,* by Irving Adler, Crowell, grades 5 up; *How Did We Find Out About Comets?,* by Isaac Asimov, Walker, grades 4–6. See also Space, pp. 147–49.

THE BODY

The study of the body is the science of physiology. Aristotle, who lived in Greece 2,500 years ago, discovered that the body has five basic senses—five completely different sensations. These are sight, sound, smell, taste and touch. Here are some experiments involving each:

Sight

OPTICAL ILLUSION: Cut from cardboard or white paper two 2-inch disks, four one-inch disks, and four 3-inch disks. Glue these to two pieces of paper the same size, each paper centered by one of the two-inch disks, combining one with the four one-inch disks (Fig. 101, A) and the other with the

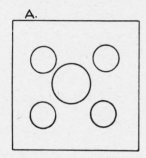
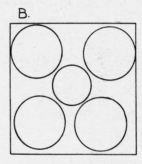

101. Optical-illusion disks.

3-inch disks (B). Hold the two papers a distance apart and ask someone which center disk is larger. The disk in A will seem larger because the eye compares it to smaller surrounding disks. The disk in B will seem smaller.

COLOR TRICKS: 1. A rainbow is white light that has been bent at different angles by round drops of water in the atmosphere. To create a rainbow, get a thick, triangular piece of glass or a prism from a chandelier, or borrow a diamond ring for a moment. Rotate the object in the sun. These prisms bend the light just as does a rainbow, making ordinary white daylight change into rainbow colors.

2. Make a top as shown (Fig. 102, A) by cutting out disks of two colors, such as blue and orange (B). Insert one into the other as shown in C and D, and spin. These will be some of the results you see: blue and orange seem white; red and green seem white; black and white seem gray; yellow and purple seem gray. These are called complementary colors (opposites). Try experimenting with other combinations.

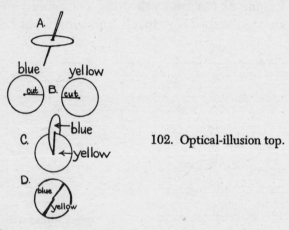

102. Optical-illusion top.

Sound

A famous puzzler is this: If an oak tree fell in a field, and there was no one—animal or man—around to hear it, would there be sound? The answer is, surprisingly, there would be no sound, because sound is merely waves of air striking hearing apparatus. Sound waves travel much like the ripples on a quiet pond when a stone is dropped into the water, in ever widening circles.

Even if someone were there, he would *see* the tree fall almost simultaneously with its actual collapse, even if some distance away, because light travels at the speed of 186,000 miles per *second*, but if he were some distance away he would not *hear* the noise until several seconds later, because sound waves travel through air at approximately one-fifth of a mile (1,100 ft.) per second. Check this by watching a bolt of lightning, and then listening for the delayed sound of its thunder. By counting the seconds slowly * you can estimate the distance it traveled.

A good test of hearing is to blindfold someone and strike two knives together to the right, to the left, in front and in back, while he tries to identify the direction. If the subject's ears are normal, he will correctly locate the right and left sounds, but confuse the front and back, because the sound is striking both ears with the same intensity. This explains why it is not always easy to locate a distant airplane in the sky.

Taste

There are four basic tastes: sweet, salty, sour, bitter. These are reported to us by the senses. Foods such as meat and eggs are none of the basic four. We feel them with the tongue. The texture, taste and smell all combine to give us flavor.

The tongue has special taste buds. When we eat we use the full tongue, but a sucker can be enjoyed more by *licking* because the sweet taste buds are at the tip of the tongue. A pill tastes bitter after it goes down because the bitter taste buds are at the back of the tongue.

EXPERIMENTS: Into a small bottle or glass squeeze some lemon juice and fill with water. Add the same amount of water to a crushed quinine tablet for a bitter sample, ¼ teaspoon sugar to water for the sweet, and a few dashes of salt to water for the salty. Use four medicine droppers or one washed well after each experiment.

---

* Most people count too rapidly to count by seconds. To time your count accurately, say "Mississippi" between each number: "one-Mississippi-two-Mississippi-three . . . ," etc.

Drop one or two drops of sugar water on the tip of the tongue, and shortly after repeat on the back of the tongue. The taste will be less sweet there and disappear sooner.

Repeat with each sample, following the chart of the tongue shown (Fig. 103). You will find that quinine, for example, has a very different taste on the front of the tongue from its

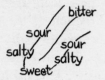

103. Taste areas of the tongue.

taste on the back. Try a very small taste of Epsom salts on the back and then on the front of the tongue. Its taste, too, you will find, depends upon its placement.

(See also "Food Experiments," p. 143.)

Touch

1. Have someone sit down, close his eyes and bend slightly forward. With two toothpicks touch him on the back of the neck, sometimes far apart, sometimes with just one. Have him indicate whether he is being touched with one or two, and where. Now try the toothpicks on the fingers, with the person still blindfolded. You will discover that the subject can identify finger touch much more accurately. Fingers have many more nerve endings than the back of the neck, because one of the purposes of the hands is to touch and identify. This experiment explains why a very tiny cut on the tip of the finger may hurt more and longer than a large, deeper scratch on the leg, for example.

2. Whenever you accidentally tear a piece of skin that must be cut away, look at it under the microscope if possible. You will see an outer scalelike layer, the epidermis, which is dead and is being constantly sloughed off. This protects the dermis,

or live skin, which can be seen underneath. The outer skin has no nerve endings. To prove this, think back:

Nearly everyone has at some time run a pin or needle through a very small, shallow area of skin. Or you may have very lightly stabbed yourself with a pin, so that the point barely pricked the surface, but hung there. You will recall that neither experience hurt. On the other hand, almost everyone can remember the pain of a "strawberry burn" on knee or elbow, received while biking or skating. The difference in degree of pain is due to the fact that the pins pricked only the epidermis, where there are no nerves, hence no feeling. The falls scraped off the protective epidermis, leaving the dermis, with its nerve endings exposed.

3. To discover why health authorities insist that thermostats (set at 65°–72°) or thermometers instead of feelings should be used to regulate the heat of a room, try these experiments:

Place a hand in a bowl of water as hot as endurable. At first it will be necessary to remove your hand once or twice. However, before the water has had time to cool greatly, the hand will be able to endure it for quite a long period. It has become accustomed to the heat, just as someone in an overheated room becomes accustomed to it.

When the hand has had time to return to its normal temperature, prepare three bowls of water: one very warm, one very cold, one lukewarm. Keep the left hand in the cold water, the right hand in the hot water, for a time. Then place both hands in the tepid water. It will feel warm to the hand from the cold water, cold to the hand from the hot water.

These experiments will explain why, when you enter a house from the outside in winter, it may feel overly warm when it is not. When coming from an overheated kitchen, the living room may feel too cool when in reality it is not. The

temptation to adjust the heat will pass as the body adjusts.
But a thermostat or thermometer cannot be fooled.

References

How the Doctor Knows You're Fine, Vicki Cobb, good
relations between doctor and child, Lippincott, grades 1–3;
*Read-and-Find-Out Science Books: How You Talk; Follow
Your Nose*, etc., Paul Showers, Crowell, grades 1–3; *The Color
of Man*, Robert Cohen, Random House, *The Many Faces of
Man*, Sharon S. McKern, Lothrop, grades 5 up.

CHEMISTRY

The entire world is made up of 92 naturally occurring
physical substances (elements), plus ten more known elements created in nuclear reactors by the breakdown of atoms.
Chemistry is the study of these elements and how they react
when combined or separated from each other. Of the thou-
sands of experiments awaiting the young scientist who wishes
to explore the science of chemistry, here are two:

Heat

Some materials are excellent conductors of heat. Some are
poor conductors. Each has a job to do. Experiment: Hold a
match against low heat on the stove. The wood of the match
will remain cool even when the match ignites and burns to
the fingers, because wood is a poor conductor of heat. Now
place an empty pan on that low heat and hold a hand flat
against the bottom for a moment. The metal pan, an excellent
conductor, gets hot almost immediately. This is one of the
reasons why cooking utensils are not made of wood—it burns
before it conducts heat—but their handles may be. This
experiment indicates the reason for many of the common
uses of wood and metal.

To discover which would make better camp drinking cups, plastic or aluminum, pour hot water into both a plastic cup and a metal measuring cup. The hot drink will immediately heat the aluminum cup, making it too hot for lip and hand. Because the cup conducts the heat *from* the liquid, the drink also cools too quickly.

Absorption

Plants draw water and food up through their trunks and stems to sustain life. To prove this, place white flowers or blossoms in water colored with bluing or food coloring.

Paper manufacturing companies use this same principle of *absorption* in deciding what type of paper to create for specific purposes. To test this, place a piece of waxed paper and a strip of paper towel or newspaper in a bowl of water. The wax coating on the one prevents water from soaking in, but paper towels are made to absorb water, and newsprint is absorbent to keep ink from smearing. Each type of paper in the house possesses its special qualities because of the job it must do, as testing will show. Test paper drinking cups, face tissues, writing paper, blotter. Type a line on high-quality typing paper, then one on mimeograph paper. Try to erase both, then dip the papers. You will find that high-quality paper is made relatively nonabsorbent to permit easy erasing. Mimeograph paper is made absorbent to hold the ink and dry quickly, and thus erases poorly.

References

A First Chemistry Book for Boys and Girls, by A. Morgan, grades 5 up; *Science Magic Tricks*, by Nathan Shalit, Holt, grades 5 up; *Cup and Saucer Chemistry*, Nathan Shalit, Grosset, grades 4–6. Also see: Science books, p. 153; General References, pp. 2–5; under Chemistry, and toy or hobby shops.

CRIME DETECTION

The brave men who served as sheriffs or marshals of the Old West would marvel at the tools that science, mostly chemistry, has given to the police, the FBI, and the sheriffs of today.

One of the most important tools is fingerprinting. Fingerprints are the result of the natural oils of the skin clinging to the surface of objects handled. The prints of no two fingers are alike; thus a careless criminal leaves a calling card when he leaves a fingerprint—a difficult thing to prevent, because wearing gloves makes the fingers clumsy.

To study this procedure, make a fingerprint powder by mixing ¼ cup of baking soda with ¼ cup or carbon (lampblack from a hardware store). Handle a dish or saucer, then sprinkle some fingerprint powder over the area, brushing very gently with a stretched-out piece of thin cotton. Gently knock off excess powder to reveal the fingerprint.

Another tool is the microscope. Carefully lay a strip of cellophane tape over the powdered fingerprint, transferring the print to the tape. Stick this to a glass microscope slide and study it. If no microscope is available use a magnifying glass, still another excellent tool. Make fingerprints of several people and compare.

For footprints, step in soft earth, then make a plaster cast (p. 173).

Photographs of the scene of the crime are another constantly used crime tool. (To study photography, see p. 115.)

Reference

Fingerprint Detective, by Robert H. Millimaki, Lippincott, grades 5 up.

FOODS

The study of foods is the science of nutrition. Scientists have discovered that man needs seven basic foods daily: (1) butter or fortified margarine; (2) citrus fruits; (3) at least two green vegetables—a green salad would count as one vegetable; (4) yellow vegetable or potatoes; (5) eggs, *whole-grain* wheat, or meat (bacon does not count); (6) one other fruit; (7) milk.

Experiments

1. Check your own diet for a full day, to see if it has included something from each group.

2. The basic foods above give us the tools of life: proteins, minerals, vitamins, fats and carbohydrates. Almost every American gets enough, and often too much, of the last two. The first three tools, proteins, vitamins and minerals, are easily destroyed or discarded if improperly handled. Nature often steers us away from unsuitable foods by making them taste less appetizing when they have lost their vital elements. Test this by these methods:

Eat some green peas, raw, the day they are purchased from the market. Leave a pod or two of the fresh peas in the refrigerator for a week, then taste. Leave a pod, plus a few peas out of another pod, on the sink counter for a few days, and taste.

The results will be surprising. If the peas were fresh and refrigerated at the store, the pods will be crisp and the peas sweet when eaten raw the first day. The peas left exposed on the counter for a few days will wither and lose both juice and taste. The pod on the counter will wither and the peas will lose flavor, as the sugar turns to starch. Even refrigerated peas kept for a week will lose some flavor—and some food value.

This experiment will produce the same results with corn, carrots, parsley, peeled potatoes and other fresh foods. In a week it will become evident that potatoes should not be peeled until used, carrots should be refrigerated and kept crisp in a plastic bag, parsley in a covered jar or plastic bag. Corn should be frozen or used in a day or two to prevent the sugar changing to starch. When foods are crisp and sweet they also contain more body builders.

3. Open an orange. Eat half immediately, leave half exposed on the counter for a day or night and then eat. The very taste of the exposed orange will indicate loss of both flavor and Vitamin C.

References

Grades 5 up: *Natural Foods*, Barbara and D. X. Fenton, Watts; *Junk Food, Fast Food, Health Food*, L. Perl, Houghton, grades 4–6: *Chains, Webs & Pyramids: The Flow of Energy in Nature*, Lawrence Pringle, and *Plants We Live On: The Story of Grains and Vegetables*, Carroll Lane Fenton and Germinie B. Kitchen, Crowell.

GEOGRAPHY

This is the study of the earth's surface—the "lay of the land." Use a long potato cut in half lengthwise to make a chart, showing the altitude of various areas (their distances above sea level).

To do this, find a topographical map in a map book or encyclopedia. It will contain circles showing the different altitudes. These are often in different colors. Now choose one small area to chart. This is especially interesting with a map of one's own area. Sometimes libraries or newspaper offices can help in this.

The full half of the potato is laid, open side down, on a sheet of paper, and the outline drawn. Remove potato and cut away a ¼-inch slice from the open side. Now lay the reduced-in-size potato in the middle of its former outline and draw its present outline (Fig. 104). Cut off as many slices

104. Altitude lines of a map, made with a potato.

as there are altitudes given in the section being charted, and draw one within the other. Label with the proper distances above sea level, as shown, or color, making a key in the corner (red for 1,000 feet, yellow for 2,000, and so on). After each tiny square of color in the key, write the altitude it represents.

(See also "Geography," p. 106, for hobby information and references.)

GEOLOGY

This is the study of how the earth beneath our feet came to be. Here is just one experiment as a starter:

When traveling or picnicking, find a road cut that exposes layers (strata) of rock, or locate an exposed rocky cliff. Study the strata. They will show how the earth is pushed and buckled to make mountains. You may be fortunate and find the fossil (rock outline) of an ancient plant or animal, even a seashell, proving that some desert or inland area was once covered with water.

With a sharp stick or penknife try to chip away the various

strata. You will find some layers that chip easily, others that are not even nicked. This will show you why rain and wind erode (carry away) the land unevenly, forming hills and gullies.

References

Grades 1–3: *How to Dig a Hole to the Other Side of the World,* Faith McNulty, Harper; *The Beginning of the Earth,* Franklin M. Branley, Crowell; grades 4–6: *The Story of Geology: Our Changing Earth Through the Ages,* Jerome Wyckoff, Golden Press; *Disastrous Volcanoes,* Melvin Berger, Watts; *The New Earth Book,* Melvin Berger, Crowell.

PERSPECTIVE

Perspective is one of the science tools of art. It is the relation between the size of an object and its distance from the eye. To understand this, go to the back door and look outside. The closest trees or buildings seem to be much taller than the trees or buildings farther away, even when they actually are the same size.

Experiments

1. Draw a railroad track or a double row of trees on a sheet of paper. Begin at the center bottom and draw the lines or trees straight to the top of the page. To check accuracy, see Fig. 105, which demonstrates the way the eye actually sees two parallel lines in the distance. The lines seem to come together because the eye is no longer able to distinguish the space between them. In drawing, such lines are not actually shown parallel, but come together at the top (the horizon) to form a long triangle, and the objects grow smaller. The next time you see a track or two rows of trees, observe them closely for perspective.

2. Sketch your back yard. Be sure to note the size of a dog, birds, fences, trees or buildings when seen close to you or to each other, as compared to those farther away.

References

Grades 4–6: *Fun with Lines and Curves,* Elsie C. Ellison, Lothrop; *Pencil, Pen and Brush: Drawings for Beginners,* Harvey Weiss, Young Scott.

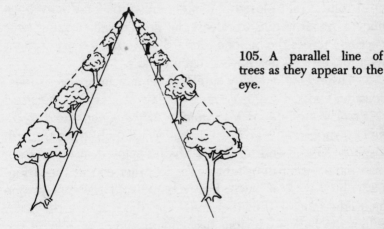

105. A parallel line of trees as they appear to the eye.

PHYSICS AND SPACE

This is the study of the unchanging laws that govern the universe. Discoveries in this one field of science have brought more changes in our knowledge in recent years than have discoveries in any other field. Consider the almost unbelievable discovery that electromagnetic impulses travel through the vacuum of space from the stars, resulting in radio, radar, TV, light, even X-rays. Consider man-made moons and shooting satellites into space, those incomprehensible distances beyond the planets, something unheard-of in human history; "One small step for man, one giant step for mankind," Neil Armstrong, Apollo Mission, first man on the moon.

Experiments

1. Here is the scientific law that makes possible the development of jets and missiles: *For every action there is a reaction*. Make a rocket to prove this.

Cut a light-weight piece of cardboard one inch square. Punch a hole in the center and push a pencil through. Through this hole pull the mouth of a long balloon; blow up until solid. Hold closed and point upward. Gradually open fingers. As air begins to release, let go. The air pushing *back* (action) forces the balloon forward (reaction). This explains why rockets and jets have streaming tails.

2. To understand why satellites remain in space so long, consider another scientific fact, the law of inertia: *Objects at rest tend to remain at rest; objects in movement tend to remain in movement*. To test this, run an 18-inch string through a spool. To one end tie a small ball, enclosed in old curtain material or other light fabric. To the other end of the string, tie a small rock or fairly heavy bolt. Hold the bolt in one hand, the spool in the other, and whirl the ball over the head. When the ball is whirling fast enough, you can release the weight, which will climb to the spool.

As long as the *speed* of the ball is balanced by the *weight* of the bolt, the ball (satellite) remains in position, because the *centripetal* force of the weight (gravity, pulling it down), is balanced by the *centrifugal* force of the ball (its inertia, causing it to keep going by flying out). When the ball whirls fast enough, its speed overbalances the bolt, pulling it up. If the whirling slows, the ball drops nearer the spool as gravity overbalances inertia. Cut the string while the ball is whirling rapidly. It will fly outward, for there is no force of gravity to balance the inertia, until its speed fails and gravity pulls it down.

Scientists have studied the speed necessary for the space satellites to balance the force of gravity *just enough* to remain "in orbit," going around the earth.

Watch trucks and cars stopping and starting at a signal to see how inertia affects all still or moving objects. Trucks, because of greater weight, both stop and start more slowly. Note, however, that even cars take considerable space and time to stop, an important fact for bicyclists and pedestrians to remember.

References

The Young Math Book Series, Crowell, grades 1–4. Grades 4–7: *A Book of Planet Earth for You* and *A Book of Outer Space for You*, Franklin Mansfield Branley, Crowell; *Biography of an Atom*, J. Bronowski and Millicent E. Salsom, Harper; *Space Scientist in Your Own Home*, Seymour Simon, Lippincott.

SOIL CONSERVATION

Soil is the pulverized rock and debris of the centuries. The topsoil is the most valuable—and the most likely to be washed away. Men until recently did not understand this or know how to prevent it, and thus a great deal of fertile land was destroyed.

To see how this happens, get two cartons of the same size from the grocery store. Cut the two sides and an end of each to three inches deep, the other end to one inch deep, (Fig. 106). Fill with about two inches of soil, packed down somewhat tightly, but molded like a hill on the shallow end, as shown (A).

On the higher end of one box (B) dig a furrow with your finger across the end and parallel to it. From this extend long furrows running straight down to the shallow end. In the other box (C) connect the same type of top furrow with another parallel to it, going across the box, and so on down to the shallow end, like a long unbroken coil, back and forth until the last parallel row curves gently to the edge.

Set each box where draining mud can be observed but will cause no damage, and tilt slightly with the deep end raised (D).

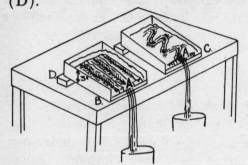

106. Soil conservation study

The miniature plowed fields are now ready for rain. Trickle a small stream of water into the higher end of each box, and compare. Either use two hoses simultaneously or time the trickling, and see which box shows more moisture by the end of perhaps three minutes. (You can also tell which holds more moisture by lifting. The soil that retains the water will be heavier.) The box with the coiled furrows (C), similar to modern contour plowing, will prove the better type in all ways: the water takes longer to pass through, causing more of it to sink in, instead of draining off, and the same box will lose less topsoil.

References

Grades 1–4: *Where Does Your Garden Grow?*, Augusta Goldin, Crowell, fruits, vegetables, trees, and flowers; *Dining on a Sunbeam*, Phyllis Busch, Four Winds. Grades 4–7: *The World Beneath Our Feet: The Story of the Soil*, Martin L. Keen, Messner; *Our Fragile Earth*, Elizabeth S. Helfman,

Lothrop; *Deserts of the World: Future Threat or Promise?*, Jane Werner Watson, Putnam.

WEATHER

Many people or organizations such as farmers and airlines need dependable weather prediction. Weathermen (meteorologists) are hoping to discover new facts about the atmosphere from our man-made satellites, in order to improve their ability to predict weather. To understand their need, try this experiment:

On a large sheet of paper, make a calendar for the current month, or use an extra one that possesses big spaces. Make the lines with colored crayon, and divide each day's square in half horizontally as in Fig. 107, with penciled lines.

107. Calendar for checking on the weatherman.

Each night read the newspaper's weather prediction for the coming day. If sunshine is predicted, draw a little sun in the *upper* half of tomorrow's square. If rain is predicted, draw raindrops or an umbrella; if cloudy, draw a cloud. Thus the upper half of each day is the *prediction*. At the end of each day, draw in the *lower* half the symbol that most nearly indicates what the weather actually was.

At the end of the month make a key in the corner. Draw each symbol used and opposite it give the number of days of each kind of weather. Below list the number of times the weatherman was wrong.

Rain Gauge

After a heavy rain there is often several inches of water in a pan left outdoors, and yet the official record may list only one inch of rainfall for the area. This is because weather stations have a gauge that measures rainfall by the amount of rain that falls in one cubic inch of space.

108. Rain gauge.

To make a fairly accurate home gauge, get a one-inch beaker, a special type of glass jar, from a chemistry, school supply or hobby shop, or a one-inch glass cigar case if no beaker is available. If it is not marked, very carefully label it with inches and quarter inches, using fine lines of nail enamel (Fig. 108). Wire the beaker to a board, leaving the holding wire loose enough to remove for emptying. Nail or wire the board to a fence post or other spot that is exposed to the sky from all sides. Check and empty after each storm.

References

I Like Weather, Aileen Fisher, Crowell, grades 1–3. Grades 4–7: *Man Changes the Weather*, Ben Bova, Addison-Wesley; *The Weather Changes Man*, Ben Bova, Addison-Wesley; *Nature's Weather Forecasters*, Helen R. Sattler, Elsevier/Nelson; *A January Fog Will Freeze a Hog, and Other Weather Folklore*, compiled by Hubert Davis, Crown, mostly folk tales and fun.

GENERAL SCIENCE REFERENCES

Appraisal, thrice-yearly children's science book reviews. Series: *Scientists at Work . . . ,* Melvin Berger, Crowell, grades 4–7; *The Reason Why Books,* Irving Adler, Crowell, grades 3–5; *Let's-Read-and-Find-Out Science Books,* Crowell, grades 1–3.

Grades 2–4: *Sending Messages,* John Warren, Houghton, speech, dance, etc.; *Science Fun for You in a Minute or Two,* Herman Schneider, McGraw-Hill; *But You Can't! Science Impossibilities to Fool You,* Vicki Cobb, Lothrop.

Grades 4 and up: *The Funny Side of Science,* Melvin Berger and J. B. Handlesman, Crowell; *Strange Mysteries from Around the World,* Seymour Simon, Four Winds; *How to Be an Inventor,* Harvey Weiss, Crowell.

Grades 5 up: *Science Experiments You Can Eat,* and *Magic . . . Naturally! Science Experiments and Amusements,* Vicki Cobb, Crowell; *How Did We Find Out About (. . . Atoms? . . . Nuclear Power?),* Isaac Asimov, Walker; *The New Earth Book: Our Changing Planet,* Melvin Berger, Crowell; *Famous Men of Science,* Sarah K. Bolton, Crowell; *Hidden Worlds,* National Geographic Society.

All ages: *Science Toys and Tricks,* Lawrence B. White, Jr., Addison-Wesley; *700 Science Experiments for Everyone,* UNESCO; *Time After Time,* Melvin Berger, Coward, how time affects us; *Inside: Seeing Beneath the Surface,* Jan Atkins, Walker, entices the eye.

NATURE LORE

*So live that in a future year, none will regret that you passed here.**

This should be the motto of the true nature lover. If you can picnic or camp or hike in the beautiful outdoors of America and *leave no record,* you will be welcome everywhere—and welcomed back. If you leave a trail of destroyed plants, paper or cans, then others truly *will* regret that you "passed here."

NATURE HOBBIES

Here are many special fields of interest for those who enjoy the outdoors, and ways of saving its treasures. For references, see Audubon Society bulletins on each special subject (address, p. 4). Other helpful organizations and books of special interest are listed on pp. 2–4.

ANIMALS

Make a collection of small animals from nature objects: cones, nuts, shells, acorns, feathers. For a beaver, see p. 110. For other ideas, using cotton, yarn and other materials, see "Animals" in Index. See also "Pets," p. 115, and "Wild Pets," p. 166.

* Adapted from a poem by Woodbridge Metcalf of the California Conservation Council.

References

Little Monsters, Jean Craig, Dial, grades 1–4; *Animals That Use Tools,* Barbara Ford, Messner, grades 3 up; *Nature's Pretenders,* Alice L. Hopf, Putnam, grades 5 up. See also Index under "Animals."

AQUARIUM

An aquarium is a balanced water-world, wherein the fish and snails take in oxygen and breathe out carbon dioxide, while the plants do the opposite.

To keep fish, such as the miniature goldfish that are the least expensive and easiest to raise, buy plant greenery for them where the fish are obtained. Add a small pinch of commercial food daily. Clean the bowl once a week by scooping out the fish with hands or dip net (p. 159) and placing them in a jar of water that has set for an hour or two—water must be room temperature. Scrub the bowl, fill with tap water and again let set. Add shells for interest, replace the greenery when eaten, and pour the fish back. Add water when it evaporates, and keep the aquarium out of the sunlight.

In a true aquarium, the plants are actually planted in an inch of sand or gravel that has been thoroughly washed free of dirt first. Lay paper over the plants to prevent uprooting, and carefully pour in water. Remove paper, wait until water is room temperature and add tadpoles, snails or fish. See: *Color Treasury of Aquarium Fish,* Crescent; and Pets, p. 115.

BIRDS

Bird watchers see many amusing and amazing sights. A mocking bird finds an 8-inch twig for its nest, and after several tries takes off like a lumbering cargo plane. A sparrow does a queer dance; he is hopping forward, scratching back—uncovering the new grass seed just planted. Sharp observation will reveal a fascinating world.

Here are a few rules for bird watching: (1) Remain quiet. (2) Move slowly. (3) Keep a distance; don't check nests unless sure they are abandoned. (4) Don't collect nests or eggs unless abandoned. (5) Make notes on the spot, to prevent forgetting or getting confused.

Points to record when possible: (1) Where the bird was seen (in a pine tree, in a meadow, etc.). (2) What it was eating. (3) How large it is, what color, what kind of bill, how it flies. (4) What is its call? (5) Was it alone or with many others? (6) Type of nest and eggs (climbing to observe may drive a mother bird away never to return, but ground nests present less of a problem).

Make a list of the points above, then look up the bird in a book (see references, below) or chart. Take books when traveling. Keep a neat, permanent notebook with your own information and notes, plus the name and page number of the book where information and pictures were found.

Bird Nests

It is possible in late fall or winter to find nests deserted by their small builders and easily seen in the bare branches. Cut out branch and all when small and not important to the tree, or remove nest with care, to prevent destruction.

Occasionally abandoned eggs can be found to fill the nests. You may discover (without observing too closely) that a long-watched back-yard nest has been deserted by the mother bird. Or eggs or parts of shells are sometimes found on the ground beneath a nest.

Since finding eggs that may be taken is a rare thing, making clay or plaster eggs (p. 10) of the proper size and painting them adds interest to the collection. See bird books for examples.

Experiments

1. Carefully pull a bird's nest apart and list the materials it contains. Study the weaving of the nest—some birds make much finer nests than others. If you already know what bird built the nest, write a description of it for your scrapbook, with other material on the same bird.

2. Plant a bird's nest in a flower pot, covering with ½ inch of dirt. Keep moist, and when it sprouts, try to identify what comes up. This reveals the needs for that type of bird, both for nesting materials and food. This information also should go into the bird notebook.

References

Wonders of Wild Ducks, Thomas D. Fegely, Dodd, Mead, grades 5 up; *Window into a Nest,* Geraldine Lux Flanagan and Sean Morris, Houghton, grades 5 up; *How Birds Fly,* Russell Freedman, Holiday House, grades 4–6; *The Birds' Woodland: What Lives There,* Coward, good identification, grades 3–6; *Look for a Bird,* Edith Thatcher Hurd, Harper, useful and beautiful, grades 1–3; a series: *Bird Talk; Birds Eat and Eat and Eat; Birds at Night; It's Nesting Time,* etc., Roma Gans, Crowell, grades 1–3.

Bird field guides can be found in the library and in book stores, or send for a list of books to the National Audubon Society, Sierra Club, and National Wildlife; for addresses see page 5.

FLOWERS

The best rule for wild flowers is to leave them as nature intended. They are becoming all too rare and fade before they can be brought home for a bouquet. For a pressed-flower scrapbook, pick them only where they are in abundance, and press immediately.

To press, place a section of newspaper on a hard surface, then wax paper, the flower, more wax paper, and finally several heavy books. When thoroughly dry, tape to a scrapbook page. When sketching, draw in the natural background: desert, forest, meadow. In the corner of page give name, if possible, and where found.

References

All ages: *Lore and Legends of Flowers*, Robert L. Crowell, Crowell; *Look at a Flower* and *State Flowers*, by Anne Ophelia Dowden, Crowell; *Wildflowers and the Stories Behind Their Names*, Phyllis S. Busch, paintings by Anne Ophelia Dowden, Scribner's; *Because of a Flower*, Loris J. Milne, Atheneum, plant/animal interrelations. See library and bookstores for field guides to flowers. National Parks have wonderful flower, animal, and tree booklets.

INSECTS

Two methods of collecting insects may be followed. The more difficult is to have sets showing the life cycle of individual insects. The second method is to collect adult insects, such as butterflies.

The easiest method of following a life cycle is to raise insects. In winter or early spring, look for cocoons, gently detach (with a section of twig if possible) and place in a half-gallon jar with a wide mouth, obtained from restaurants. Punch several air holes in the lid.

One day an adult insect will emerge. If it is a female, it wi'l lay eggs in the jar. Watch for this. Egg-laying occurs within several hours after she emerges from the chrysalis.

When caterpillars emerge from the eggs, around two

weeks, begin to drop a few leaves into the jar. Experiment to find the types preferred. Begin with those of plants closest to the place where the cocoon was obtained.

Constant feeding should produce at least a few caterpillars which survive all the skin changes and other hazards, to change, in about two months, back into the pupa stage, which also lasts around two months, thus completing the life cycle.

Butterfly Net

To catch butterflies and moths, find a bamboo pole (best because it is light), or other long stick such as a broom handle. Bend a wire clothes hanger into a circle, and straighten the curved hanger-top. Cut a piece of mosquito netting, cheesecloth or old net curtains 38 by 40 inches.

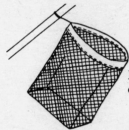

109. Butterfly net. In miniature, this can be a dip net.

Across the top (a 38-inch end) stitch a border of wide mending tape. Double the material and stitch down the side. Stitch the bottom hem to a 12-inch square of similar material. Sew the taped top over the wire loop, attach the straightened top of the hanger to the pole with wire, and the butterfly net is complete (Fig. 109).

References

A First Look at Insects, Millicent Salsam and Joyce Hunt, Walker, grades 2–4; How Insects Communicate, Dorothy Hinshaw Patent, Holiday House, grades 4–7; The Milkweed and Its World of Animals, Ada Graham, Doubleday, grades 5 up; The Bug Clan, Dodd, grades 5 up.

ROCKS

Rock Collection

A rock collection can be just a group of rocks, but it is more interesting to read about the rocks in books and learn to identify the collection by type. Rocks can be grouped by their natural location (Rocky Mountain rocks), or by their type (igneous, sedimentary, metamorphic).

Try to keep the specimens as near the same size as possible to add uniformity to the collection. Mount on heavy corrugated paper cut from cartons and painted, or in plaster of Paris casts (p. 173), or in boxes, by cementing. Before cementing, use a fine brush or toothpick to paint a number on the rock in India ink, white enamel or nail enamel. On a label below the mounting, or in the lid of the box, or on a separate chart, opposite that same number list these facts when possible: the name of the rock, the type, where and when found, and uses.

Rocks can be collected also to illustrate the geology of the world. One rock might expose a particularly interesting bit of strata (layers showing the passage of time just as tree rings do). Another might show water erosion, or an imbedded fossil.

Look for a lapidary store in your area where stones may be seen and identified. This will help identify the specimens in your collection.

References

The Rock-Hound's Book, Seymour Simon, Viking, grades 6 up; *Album of Rocks and Minerals,* Tom McGowan, Rand McNally, grades 4 up; *The National Audubon Society Field Guide to North American Rocks and Minerals,* Charles W. Chesterman, Knopf, all ages. See also Geology, p. 146, and Geography, p. 106.

THE SEA AND SHELLS

Skin diving and glass-bottom boats may not be within everyone's reach, but many movies have been made showing the wonders of the sea. Watch for these. Keep a scrapbook. Make drawings of seaweed and collections of shells (below). Become a beachcomber, looking for interesting deadwood, glass fragments and other objects washed up by the sea.

Shell Collection

The best time to collect shells is when the tide is far out, or in the early morning before the beach has been picked clean of unusual varieties.

Shells can be mounted with household cement on heavy corrugated paper cut from a carton and painted or covered. They can be mounted on a thin board, or "free" form such as a flat piece of driftwood. Small shells can be kept in molded egg cartons. They can be grouped by related families, such as varieties of clams, or by locations where found, such as Oregon Coast, or Gulf Coast.

Write or paste in, below each shell, its name when possible, and where and when found. (To mount in plaster of Paris, see p. 173.)

References

Shells Are Skeletons, Joan Berg Victor, Crowell, grades 1–3; *Houses from the Sea,* Alice E. Goudey, Scribner's, grades 1–3; *Creative Shellcraft,* Katherine N. Cutler, Lothrop, grades 4–6; *Color Treasury of Sea Shells,* Crescent, all ages. Libraries, bookstores, and shell stores have guides on regional shells.

TREES

If trees are taken for a hobby, a scrapbook of pictures or drawings can be made, or separate collections, such as woods, leaves, twigs, seeds, can be made. Or each tree may be taken individually with everything pertaining to it displayed on one card.

Make cards of equal size from grocery-store cartons; around 8 by 10 inches is a satisfactory size. Sketch a picture of the tree in one corner, or cut one from a magazine; paste down. Sketch the blossom if possible. Then, to the same piece of cardboard, cement a sample of wood, a twig, a leaf, seeds and seed pods, cones, etc. Label with the name of the tree, tell where found, give uses.

To study trees, learn to recognize different types by the following: leaves, twigs, way of branching, size, place of growth, fruits, blossoms, berries, nuts or cones, bark.

Learn the uses of trees: for man, as food, fuel, building material, paper, or other products; for animals, as food or shelter (beavers, for example, use trees for food *and* shelter); and for plants, as shelter or soil conditioner. Make sketches of leaves, tree products, and the trees themselves, for the tree scrapbook.

See "Nature Crafts," p. 167, for things to do with leaves, bark, etc.

Leaf Collection

Leaves should be pressed to make a good collection. Place leaves on five or six sheets of newspaper on a board or other flat surface, cover with newspaper, top with another flat surface and weigh down heavily with books or rocks.

When thoroughly dry, tape or glue the leaves to a scrapbook page or piece of cardboard. Paste a label beneath, or write in the name of the tree, where found, its type and uses. If possible, sketch a picture of the tree. To glue to slick surfaces such as oilcloth or glass, use a mixture of glue and vinegar in equal parts, pressing until dry.

LEAF PRINTS: These may be made in a number of ways.

1. Wax mounting: Press fresh-picked colored leaves between two sheets of heavy wax paper, using a warm iron, then mount in a scrapbook with tape or glue.

2. Crayon print: Place a section of newspaper or a magazine on a work area to give a soft surface. Lay the leaf on this with the underside (vein side) up. Over this place thin drawing paper, hold carefully, and color the leaf area solidly with the side or flat end of a soft crayon, choosing green or other autumn leaf colors. Make all strokes go in the same direction. Cut out along the leaf outline and mount in a scrapbook.

3. Ink print: Cut a piece of felt the size of the largest leaf on hand. Place felt on a board or glass and carefully pour on some ink until well-moistened. Place leaf on this, vein-side down, cover with heavy paper and run a hand or roller over it carefully. Then lift the leaf, being *very* careful not to smear, place it on plain paper, and again roll or press. Be sure to permit thorough drying. If ink printing is well done, it is the best type for a scrapbook because it shows veining so clearly. Tubes of printer's ink from a stationery store are best for this, but not necessary. Green is the best color.

4. Clay print: For this, use a perfect, wide, attractive leaf such as maple. Use a permanent type (p. 11) of clay (from stationery store or hobby shop) that needs no kiln-drying for a lasting print. Roll out a piece of clay ¼-inch thick and at least as large as the leaf to be cast. Lay the leaf on the clay, vein-side down, and roll carefully with rolling pin or dowel stick, then cut out the outline of the leaf with a knife or a paper clip opened out. Carefully curl the edges of the clay to resemble a real leaf, and then place rolls of clay under the curled edges to hold in position while drying. Cover with a damp cloth to permit even drying. When thoroughly dry

(several days later), paint with art enamel from a stationery store. This makes an attractive candy dish.

5. Spatter print: Place newspaper over work area. Lay the paper to be spattered on cardboard, and pin the leaf flat to this, pins upright. Leaf prints are more successful if the leaf has been pressed for an hour or two.

Prepare poster paint the consistency of thin cream, dip an old toothbrush into the mixture, press against the side of the can to remove excess paint, and rub toothbrush *toward you* on a small piece of clean window screening held over the leaf. In this way spatter paint onto the paper all around the leaf. When dry, remove leaf, leaving a clear design.

Seed Collection

A seed collection can include not only the seeds but their protectors: cones, pods, thistles, "parachutes," and "wings."

Place the seeds themselves in the center of a small piece of transparent plastic paper. Fold up to form an envelope, seal the three open sides with tape and attach the top with tape to a cardboard, with a label to identify the seed and tell where found. On this same card glue the seed protector. If the tree or plant has been observed through the seasons, sketch pictures of the stages of development. With a peach seed, for example, show the spring blossom and summer fruit from which the seed came.

Twig Identification

Identifying twigs of deciduous trees (those that lose their leaves in winter) takes care and study. The best time to collect is in late winter or early spring. Label each twig when collected, to prevent mixing them. Cut off two 6-inch tips, cutting at a sharp angle to expose the interior better.

Tie or plastic-tape one twig of each type of tree to the twig collection cardboard, or to the tree collection (p. 161). Place the other twig in deep water. If possible, sketch the buds and leaves as the twig in water begins to open, and place this with the twig from the same tree. An Audubon Society leaflet and chart will teach identification of twigs (for address, see p. 4). A few comparisons will quickly show how even "dead" branches differ.

WOOD COLLECTIONS: When dead branches are available, choose bark-covered samples of various woods that are perhaps one inch around, 5 inches long. Cut the sample halfway

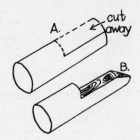

110. Wood cut to show the grain.

down through the center and slice off as shown (Fig. 110, A) to display the grain. On the sliced end make a slanting cut as shown (B), to show the quarter grain. Sandpaper and shellac the cut surfaces.

Thumbtack a card to the piece of wood, stating type, uses, where found. Or glue the wood into a box with card pasted beneath.

If dead branches cannot be found, park rangers or others in charge may be able to supply cuttings of live wood. In this case the cutting must be seasoned by permitting it to dry thoroughly, before adapting it to a collection.

WILD PETS

It is difficult to keep wild pets, which seldom eat well in captivity. It is better to observe them a few days and then release them.

References: Grades 1–3: *The Zoo in My Garden,* Chiyoko Nakatani, Crowell; to observe: *Big Tracks, Little Tracks,* Franklyn M. Branley, Crowell. Grades 5–8: *Shelf Pets: How to Take Care of Small Wild Animals,* Edward R. Ricciuti, Crowell.

Earthworms

Use a pint jar with a wide mouth and a lid punched with holes. When not observing, place in a brown paper bag and fasten the bag with a rubber band to the rim of the jar. Spread the bag open above the rubber band and cut the top off about two inches above the lid.

Nearly fill the jar with moist, loosely packed earth and perhaps four earthworms. For food place bits of bread dipped in milk, leftover oatmeal or mashed potatoes at the top. Change the food daily.

To observe, take the jar from the bag. Watch the growth of the worms and see why they are called the farmer's friends, as they push through the earth, "plowing," and permitting air to enter.

Tadpoles (Polliwogs)

To catch tadpoles, minnows or other small water animals, make a dip net, following instructions for a butterfly net (p. 159) in a miniature size, about 4 inches around and 5 inches deep. Take also a can or small bucket, because they should be kept in the water in which they were found. To make a handle for the can, punch holes opposite each other near the rim and tie a string handle.

Bring home scum, sticks and plants with the animals. Place in a large jar or aquarium. When the tadpoles become frogs they need a stone or stick protruding from the water, or a cork, to rest on, and bits of lettuce for food.

When they turn into frogs free them or place in a terrarium (p. 171). They need flies, insects and meat bits to eat, but since they catch moving food, it should be suspended on tweezers or thread and moved.

NATURE CRAFTS

Diorama

A diorama is a scene built into a box. Use a small wooden box such as a prune box from the grocery store, or sturdy cardboard boxes of small size, or half-gallon ice cream containers. Cut one side and the top away. With the ice cream container, cut away a third of the side but none of the bottom.

111. Diorama.

For the floor surface use real moss or lichen, sand, plaster of Paris (p. 10), papier-mâché (p. 10), or clay (p. 11), real grass, Easter grass. Bits of sponge, especially if colored already or dried with colored poster paint in them, serve as bushes (or see p. 72). Use glass as water; place blue or green

paper beneath, and place clay, grass or other substance over
the edge to give natural, uneven borders. Use rocks and pebbles for boulders. Rather thick twigs can serve as logs or
bridges. For tents, see p. 56; for matchstick cabins, see p. 90.
Trees can be miniature toys from the five-and-ten, or shellac-
sprayed evergreen bits, or see p. 72. Animals, fences, human
figures, boats, cars, and so on, all can be toy miniatures or
pipe-cleaner figures (p. 74). The surface can be painted to
resemble grass sprayed with Christmas snow. The walls of
the carton can be painted to resemble a blue sky, perhaps
with scudding clouds, painted white or made of thin cotton
(Fig. 111).

Shadow Boxes

CIGAR BOX: This is a variety of textured painting (p. 23).

Ask a druggist to save a flat, one-inch-deep cigar box. Tear
off the paper or cover with a damp cloth *just* long enough to
remove paper. When dry, sand lightly if necessary. Paint the
outside a color to harmonize with the room in which it will
hang. Paint the inside blue (for sky).

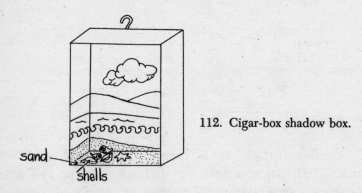

112. Cigar-box shadow box.

Draw a design on paper first, to prevent errors. Plan the
scene to suit miniature nature objects that are easily col-

lected. For example, moss or lichen (from woods or hobby shop), small twigs, some pebbles, sand, can provide materials for a picture of a tree (twig for trunk, lichen for leaves), a stream with real sand sprinkled on glue at the edge, with the pebbles as rocks (see Fig. 112). A bridge can be made of twigs, flowers of crepe paper (p. 31). Miniature shells can be used for a shore scene. Each item is glued to floor or back. Objects needed for the scene may be made from papier-mâché (p. 10) or crepe or craft paper.

SARDINE-CAN SHADOW BOX: Use a sardine can of any type. This can be painted first if desired, for added color. Glue a piece of blue craft paper to the inside bottom, or paint blue, for background. To this background glue tiny sprigs of dried grains or grasses, seed pods, etc., in a pleasing arrangement (Fig. 113).

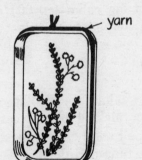

yarn

113. Sardine-can shadow box.

Run a piece of rug yarn or braided wool yarn (p. 97) around the outside rim and tie at the top, with which to hang the box. If desired, a small piece of plastic paper such as Saran Wrap can be placed over the box as "glass." The yarn can be tied over this to hold it.

Small shadow boxes are even more attractive if hung in pairs or fours with different arrangements in each.

Bark Scene

Create a woodland scene by using thick, interesting pieces of bark, twigs, mosses such as spagnum, lichens, or small rocks.

Turn the rough side of the bark up as a base. Use blue poster paint to create a winding stream. Glue small twigs upright as dead or winter-bound trees, or glue moss or colored sponge bits to the twigs for green trees. Add bits of

114. Bark scene.

moss or small rocks for interest. Imagination will supply many other ideas, such as adding a small log cabin (p. 90) or tepee (p. 112), miniature plastic animals, or a beaver dam of tiny twigs (Fig. 114).

Woodland Tracks

To keep a permanent record of the animal tracks that are so exciting to find, take supplies for making plaster casts when traveling. A shoebox or lunch pail will hold cardboard and paper clips, or low cans such as tuna and deviled ham come in, for frames; also: plaster of Paris powder, a tin can, Vaseline, and talcum. Carry a canteen of water.

When a track is found, cut a one-inch strip of cardboard long enough to circle the track, clip ends together with a paper clip, and press gently into the earth, to hold the mold. Or cut both ends from a low can large enough to circle the track and press it into the ground. Lightly sprinkle the track with talcum.

Use a tin can to mix plaster of Paris with water (p. 10) to the consistency of cream; add a pinch of salt if in a hurry, and carefully pour over the track. This will harden in ten minutes. Then the mold can be removed and the cast cleaned. It is now like a negative of a photograph—just backward. To make a positive cast, coat the negative cast with Vaseline and circle it with a new cardboard or can frame. Again pour plaster over it. When this hardens, there will be an exact print of the track to add to your home museum.

Terrarium

This is a miniature garden under glass. Use an aquarium or a wide-mouth gallon glass jar from a restaurant. If a jar is used, lay it on its side and make a frame to prevent rolling. This can be two narrow strips of wood nailed parallel to each other on a board, with just enough room between them to rest the jar. Paint the base for neatness.

A terrarium can be made of woodland or bog plants, desert or cultivated ones. It should be arranged as a scene. First bits of gravel or broken flower pots are scattered, then sand into which charcoal is pressed. Over this sprinkle one or two inches of the type of soil the particular plants require. This can be built into "hills" for interest. Rocks can be added for boulders, a small glass dish with pebbles in it for a pool. A desert terrarium will of course contain mainly sand, plus cacti from the five-and-ten.

The plants should be placed far enough apart to avoid crowding. Native insects or animals (lizards, baby frogs) may be added. Water preferably with a fine spray. Since a terrarium has a lid, usually one that permits some air to enter, however, watering is needed very infrequently, possibly only once a month. When a slight mist clings to the glass the terrarium has enough water.

For complete instructions, write to National Audubon Society (address p. 4) for *The Terrarium*, 15¢.

Nature Jewelry

String nature items together on a wire or heavy cord, long enough to permit the hand to squeeze through, for a bracelet, or to go over the head for a necklace. Use acorn or eucalyptus cups, small nuts or acorns, tough seed pods, shells. Follow a pattern, such as placing two acorn cups back to back, followed by a small acorn, and repeating.

Map Making

Sketch a map of an area while looking down on it from a hill, or map a trail or your home area while walking.

Be consistent in the use of symbols, using the same symbol for the same feature each time, such as two lines running closely parallel for streams, one line for roads, etc. Proportions should be as accurate as possible. In a lower corner, make a "legend," showing the sign used for each feature.

Reed Basket

Soak reeds (found in marsh or hobby shop) in water for one half hour, then lay four one-foot reeds on a table. Lay five one-foot reeds on top in the other direction, as shown (Fig. 115, A). Run a long reed around these "warp" reeds, under all four, over all five (B), pressing close together as you work. Begin a second reed where the first ends. On the fifth full round, spread the reeds in a sunburst as you weave, going over one reed, under the next (C). Reeds and basket should be dipped in water frequently as the work progresses, to prevent breaking. See finished basket (D). Glue down the last 2 inches of the top row to prevent unraveling.

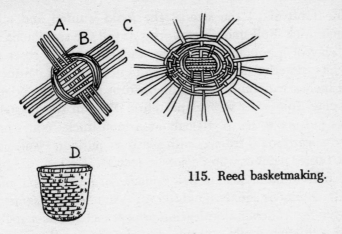

115. Reed basketmaking.

Ink Prints

See p. 163 for method. In addition to leaves, fern fronds and flowers can be ink-printed, preferably after pressing for an hour or two. If printer's ink is used, clean the glass with turpentine when finished. Printer's ink is not washable, so protect clothes.

Toys to Make

Use cones, seeds, nuts, acorns, pods, twigs, feathers, for materials. Create animals, men, birds, trees, plants. Hold together with picture wire, pipe cleaners, glue or household cement. This is an excellent party craft.

Plaster of Paris Casts and Mounts

Casts may be made of animal tracks (p. 170), leaves, ferns, flowers, twigs, seeds, rocks or shells. For collections, if it is desired to mount more than one specimen on one cast, all specimens must be on hand when the mold is made, for plaster hardens fast and cannot be remolded.

To make casts, roll out on paper some "five-and-ten" Plas-

ticine (soft clay) the size of the mold wanted and about
½-inch thick. Roll smooth and press or roll the specimens into
the clay deeply enough to show veins, fern spore cases and
the like. Remove the specimens and cut a piece of cardboard
two inches wide and long enough to fit around the edge of
the clay. Join ends with paper clips. Pour in the plaster of
Paris (to make, see p. 10) about ½ inch thick. When hard,
remove cardboard frame, wash plaster (outdoors) and paint
with poster paint or water colors if desired.

If individual molds are being made for a collection, make
small circular or square molds of approximately the same size
to give the collection a pleasing appearance. Press a rock or
shell into each while still wet and do not handle until set.
To label, see "Rocks," p. 160.

Seed Mosaic

On a square piece of cardboard draw a simple scene or a
design, as in Fig. 116. Get a variety of any seeds from a pet
or feed store, being sure they are packaged separately. Only

116. Seed mosaic.

a handful is necessary of each kind: sunflower seed, barley,
wheat, bird seed. Coat with a layer of glue all parts of the
design to be covered with one type of seed. Arrange large
seeds individually, or sprinkle small ones. When this is dry,
repeat with another part of the design, and so on until it is
covered.

Bean Mosaic

A colorful mosaic for a wall decoration, map making or other designs can be made of a variety of dried beans, glued to a background of thin plywood or heavy cardboard. Draw the design lightly in pencil and fill in the outlines with a thin layer of glue, then beans, as shown in Fig. 117.

117. Bean mosaic.

If other colors are desired, such as blue for water, white rice or lima beans may be colored by placing in water tinted with food coloring until the desired shade is obtained. Dry before gluing. Rice spreads quickly with the back of a spoon.

HIKES AND FIELD TRIPS

A hike is a brisk walk, with walking the main point. A field trip means going slowly enough to see everything of special interest. On any field trip keep a sharp eye open for craft, decoration or collection items to bring home: seeds and cones, cattails and reeds, interesting deadwood branches and bark, rocks and moss. (Take *nothing* from a national park.)

Take any equipment that might be needed: a shoulder bag

for finds, including small jars or cans with tight lids for water samples, lids with holes for insects or other animals, a notebook and pencil to record information, molding equipment for track records (p. 170). The equipment will depend on your aims.

Reference

In Woods and Fields, by Margaret Buck, Abingdon (ten years and up).

Reminders: Leave gates as found. Stay out of farmed fields. Obey "No Trespassing" signs. Do not permanently mark a trail (with broken limbs, for example). Remain quiet to hear natural sounds.

Marshlands and Ponds

Before investigating these, check for good footing, to avoid sucking mud.

Since marshes and ponds are usually still water, they are particularly good sources for animal and plant study. Take home samples of scum and water to study under a microscope. Look for fowl-life in particular. Observe whether there are ducks, geese, mud fowl or other water lovers such as cranes and killdeers. Try to discover whether they are nesting or migrating; observe how they group themselves for flying.

Look for cattails and long reeds to bring home. The latter may be used for basket-making or mats (p. 172).

The Farm

See what different animals are fed, where they are kept, how they care for their young. Why is the farmer raising them?

Observe the field crops. How are they planted, how cared

for, when harvested? What will the product be used for (frozen foods, truck marketing, seed, canning, animal food)?

Find out which wild animals the farmer likes, which are pests. How does he care for the soil to prevent erosion (see "Soil Conservation," p. 149) and retain fertility?

Bring home dried weeds and seed pods for flower arrangements.

When visiting on a farm, you will find that dawn and twilight are the most interesting times.

The River

Climb a hill to observe how a river flows: note the direction, the current as the river widens and narrows, the land surrounding it, the riffles and curves. Observe what the river does to its banks by studying levees, trees and man-made protectors.

Walk along the bank and look for water and sand animals and plants, deadwood, erosion marks and tide marks. Watch for jumping fish. In the fall keep a lookout in the shallow waters near the banks for schools of baby fish migrating after spawning. Watch insects light on the water without breaking the surface tension.

Try to catch small river animals—crabs, polliwogs, crayfish, fish; fix a tub with river plants and water if possible and experiment with raising them. Feed them insects, bits of meat and lettuce, fish food.

If there is a waterfall, study what the force of the water is doing to the rocks above and below; discover why it is so powerful.

The Beach

The best time for a beach walk is at low tide. Tennis shoes are helpful for climbing around rocks. Beach park officers, the city hall of a beach town, the local newspaper or an almanac can provide the time when an unusually low tide is expected. Things to look for: water and dune plants, water and sand animals and birds and the tracks they make, shifting sand, tide marks, the effect of water on rocks and pebbles. Small pools caught in the rocks when the tide goes out may contain a great deal of sea life to be observed. Collect shells and driftwood and water-molded glass. From a dune or hill observe color changes in the water.

Lakes

If possible, observe from a hill. Try to discover why the water is there. Find the river or stream that feeds it, and one that carries its waters away.

Walk along the shore and look for animal tracks, deadwood, native plants and animals, trees that hug the water. Watch the wind create swells and whitecaps. Observe how small lagoons and inlets are protected. See the color of the water change with the weather, the time of day, the depth of the water.

Try to discover reasons why the water is pure and clean, or murky and dirty. Test the water and try to discover reasons why it is warm or cold. Float sticks to test the current and, when you find a current, look for a reason why one should exist at that point.

Dams

If a dam is nearby, find out the reason for its existence: for safety, for a city water supply, for irrigation or a fish refuge.

If it is a large dam, walk across if permitted. Try to picture reasons why the engineers built it in that particular place, why that special height and thickness was necessary.

Some dams have fish ladders, like giant steps up the side, for fish going upstream to spawn (lay eggs). Discover how the ladders operate, and in autumn watch, if possible, as the fish jump them. See how specialized animals such as eels manage. In the spring watch for baby fish.

Mountains and Forests

These areas abound in trees, ferns, mosses and unusual rock formations to observe. Watch for native birds or glimpses of wild animals. Locate burrows, nests, tree holes of squirrels or birds, honey trees. Look under rocks, logs, or loose bark for insects. Study the life rings of a tree stump. Compare trees to discover the varieties of the same family, such as pine.

Where the ground is moist look for animal tracks. Dig up a bit of soil with a stick and see the layers of rich humus that the trees are giving to the earth.

See how rivers and streams and waterfalls change the face of the land. Study exposed rock formations that show how the soil was laid down in strata, layer by layer, then crushed into hard rock, and then perhaps tilted as the mountains were formed, eons ago.

Make animal track molds (p. 170). Bring home rocks, cones, bark, twisted branches, leaves, feathers, for crafts, collections, or decoration.

Meadows and Fields

Unplowed fields and meadows are the best areas to look for wild grasses and flowers, for insects and small field animals such as gophers and ground squirrels. Observe ground-loving birds such as field owls and meadowlarks. Try to spot burrows and nests without disturbing them.

For a collection or "everlasting" arrangement, look for

dried grasses, thistles and seed stalks or flowers in abundance, pretty rocks or interesting twigs.

Around a City Block

Even if mountains, beach or country are inaccessible, there is a world of nature in your own yard and block. Develop the habit of *seeing* what goes on around you: how the trees change with the seasons; how grass and weeds push up toward the light, even through the driveway asphalt; what wild animals such as birds and squirrels brave the presence of man in your neighborhood.

Learn to ask questions: Why are certain types of plants grown so commonly in the area? Why do big trees crack the concrete around them? Why are flies drawn to the house?

One Aim

If there is a favorite spot near your home, or there is enough time at a farm or vacation area to cover the same trail more than once, specialize in what to observe. On one trip count the varieties of trees, get leaf samples, compare their bark and what uses they have. Perhaps you can discover the pests, or the flowers or birds that favor that environment. On other trips study and collect insects, or spend the time bird watching.

NATURE, ECOLOGY, AND ENVIRONMENT REFERENCES

Series: *Books for Young Explorers*, National Geographic Society, the natural world, grades 1–5; *A First Look at ...* (*... Insects; ... Plants*, etc.). Millicent E. Selsam et al., Walker, grades 1–4. Grades 1–3: *I Stood upon a Mountain* (Caldecott award, Blair Lent), and *Out in the Dark and Daylight*, nature verse, both by Aileen Fisher, Crowell; *Poetry of Earth*, Adrienne Adams, Scribner's; *Walk with Your Eyes* and *Touch Will Tell*, Marcia Brown, Watts; *The Sunlit Sea* and

The Bottom of the Sea, Augusta Goldin, Crowell; *A Walk in the Snow*, Phyllis S. Busch, Lippincott; *How to Be a Nature Detective, Hidden Animals* (camouflage), and *Greg's Microscope*, Millicent E. Selsam, Harper; *The Earth Book*, Gary Jennings, Lippincott; *Forest Log*, James R. Newton, Crowell; *Mr. Jameson & Mr. Phillips*, Marjorie Weinman Sharmat, Harper.

Grades 3–6: *Like and Unlike: A First Look at Classification*, Solveig Paulson Russell, Walker; *Grocery Store Botany*, Joan Elma Rahn, Atheneum, experiments; *Nature Games & Activities*, Sylvia Cassell, Harper; *Play with Seeds*, Millicent E. Selsam, Morrow, experiments.

Grades 4–6: *The Blossom on the Bough: A Book of Trees* and *Look at a Flower*, Anne O. Dowden, Crowell; *Metamorphosis: The Magic Change*, Alvin Silverstein, Atheneum; *The Curious Naturalist*, John Mitchell et al., Prentice-Hall, crafts and experiments; *The Organic Living Book*, Bernice Kohn, Viking; *Nature Crafts*, Carol Inouye, Doubleday; *From Petals to Pinecones: Nature Art & Craft Book*, Katherine A. Cutler, Lothrop; *Collect, Print and Paint from Nature*, John Hawkinson, Whitman; *The New Water Book*, Melvin Berger, Crowell, experiments; *To the Brink of Extinction*, Edward R. Ricciuti, Harper; *Mice, Moose and Men*, Robert M. McClung, Morrow; *Plants & Insects Together*, Dorothy Hinshaw Patent, Holiday House; *Shadows over the Land*, Joseph J. McCoy, Seabury; *Poisoned Land*, Irene Kiefer, Atheneum; *Man's Mark on the Land*, Arthur S. Gregor, Scribner's; *Whale Watch*, Ada and Frank Graham, Delacorte; *The Wind Is Round*, Sara Hannum and John T. Chase, Atheneum, verse, "discover our Eden"; *The Seeing Eye*, Victor B. Scheffer, Scribner's, photos.

See also: *Ranger Rick's Nature Magazine*, National Wildlife Federation, 1412 16th Street N.W., Washington, D.C. 20036, pocket guides (birds, butterflies).

CONVALESCENCE

There are many suggestions given below to make convalescence a time of entertaining and worthwhile activity. A number of the ideas may be carried out alone by the convalescent, giving the family the opportunity to help when possible, without spoiling him by constant attention.

PRACTICAL HINTS

If the illness is contagious, use newspaper or paper bags for waste, gay paper plates, paper craft articles (p. 77) that can be burned. A large market bag can be hung on the edge of the mattress to catch scraps from play.

Bedside.Table

If no table is available, use a card table or orange crate gaily covered. Keep necessaries handy: tissues, lotions, a damp washcloth in a dish to wipe hands during craft work. It is comforting to have a bell to call for assistance and a clock to keep track of time, plus a play clock (p. 194) for younger children set at a special time. ("When the clock hands reach here, Jimmy will be home.")

Simple Food Surprises

MILK SIPPERS: Occasionally use straws with gay faces. The convalescent can make one-inch disks of white paper or cardboard and draw his own faces, or flowers, or toys, then glue these to straws for himself and the other children.

CLOWN: Use a scoop of ice cream, a cone tipped on top for a hat, candies for eyes and mouth, a doilie on the plate as a ruff.

FLOWER SALAD: Place a rounded scoop of cottage cheese in the center, surrounded by pineapple chunks as petals. Embed five or six raisins in the center of the cottage cheese.

SUNSHINE SALAD: The same as the flower salad, omitting the raisins.

CANDLE DESSERT: Stand half a banana upright in a slice of pineapple. Cut a shallow groove on top for a marachino cherry "flame." The handle can be a marshmallow, a Lifesaver candy, a nutmeat or a pineapple chunk.*

Visitors

If the convalescent is well enough and his illness is not contagious, he might have a small friend in for lunch or even dinner. Parents should watch the patient for signs of fatigue and permit only one or two visitors at a time.

When friends or relatives want to bring something or to help, a "sunshine box," might be suggested. This is a box of individually wrapped trinkets, to be opened, perhaps, at stated times.

Protector

Use soft plastic to cover bedclothes for messy craft work.

Back Rest

Pillows slip and tire the back. If convalescence is to be long, buy a beach back rest, or put a straight chair upside

* For suggestions on children's nutrition in general, see *Let's Have Healthy Children*, by Adelle Davis, Harcourt, Brace.

down under the mattress, the latter resting against the sloping chair back. Or use a board inclined against the headboard. Place a pillow under the knees.

Book Holder

Buy one, or make by bending a wire coat hanger and hanging it over a tray tilted against knees or pillow.

Toys

There should be many, all easily workable. They should be practical for bed play. Avoid overly messy types or those with small parts that may get lost. This is the time for the box of toys put away because they had grown too familiar, or the Christmas overflow. This is the time for the kaleidoscope, the viewer with colored film transparencies, the blackboard and magic slate; for board games, especially those of pure chance that permit an imaginary opponent. Save old magazines, catalogues, cardboard and scraps of all kinds, for crafts and other play.

Shoe Bag

Pin one to the edge of the mattress or across the headboard to hold small, constantly used items.

Change of Scene

If not too ill or suffering from a contagious disease, the closer the convalescent is to the center of things, the happier he will be.

Writing Board

Purchase at a large drug or stationery store. Use for writing or to hold book or craft materials.

Activity Tray

To prevent small toys, pegs, etc., from getting lost in a game, make an activity tray. Get a medium-size carton with an uncut lid. Remove lid, cut the sides down to about 3 inches from the bottom, dipping to one inch on the side that will face the convalescent. Place the flat lid, smooth side up, in the bottom of the box. This permits play with miniature toys or other games that require flat, unbroken surfaces. The tray can then be removed as set up, for later play. A larger box can be used to make a flat surface for board games.

Entertainment

Members of the family should take turns carrying in trays to the convalescent, as well as running errands, reading, and so on, for variety.

Make a "surprise ball" (p. 47) for the convalescent, and later have him make one for a friend.

The convalescent will enjoy things to watch: a dish garden, a fish, a bird if patient is not allergic to it. A bed placed near a window permits bird watching (see p. 155). A bird feeder or birdhouse outside the window makes this easier.

Use string across a wall for pinning up craft articles, interesting pictures, maps. A bulletin board made of wallboard from a lumberyard can hold get-well cards and other treasures. Make a flannel board (p. 187) for play. Use a card table for supplies of crafts and so on. Clear it each night, however, so that everything will seem new daily. Make a bed table of boards between chairs, or use a stiff cardboard box with knee space cut out. Cover with oilcloth. (A real bed table is worth buying or making if the illness is long.)

When there are several pieces of mail, deliver one at a time, at mailtime, lunchtime, etc.

RADIO AND TV: A bedside radio is a great source of comfort, especially to an older convalescent who may wish to learn words to the songs his friends are singing. One or two carefully chosen TV shows spaced throughout the day will give something to anticipate.

Schoolwork

If the convalescent is able to work, the teacher will help with suggestions to keep up on his schoolwork, and there are workbooks for various age levels. Reference books such as an encyclopedia set (see p. 3) are invaluable. He might learn to type: the hunt-and-peck system if under ten, copying hand-printed words, if very young. For an older convalescent a book can be borrowed from a nearby junior or senior high school that will teach the touch-typing system.

Even a very small child can profit from foreign-language lessons from a high school or college neighbor, and foreign-language records are available at some libraries.

PLAY IDEAS

Getting well is usually a quiet time, and the play ideas given below are for just such times.*

Here also are some suggestions especially suitable for convalescent periods: Work on collections or hobbies. Make decorations and crafts for a holiday coming up. Make scrapbooks (p. 95) or mobiles (p. 38). Bring the family photograph albums up to date. The convalescent can write to friends; listen to radio or phonograph or watch TV—not more than one or one and a half hours a day; learn to sew (p. 117), weave (p. 127), embroider, knit, crochet, braid (p. 97), or do needlepoint.

* See also: "Crafts," "Nature Lore," "Fun with Science," "Hobbies."

Flannel Board

Buy a light-weight plywood board or wallboard from a lumberyard, 18 by 24 inches, plus light green outing flannel to cover, with two inches to spare all around (22 by 28 inches). Pull the cloth neatly over board and thumbtack behind.

The flannel board may be used to tell picture stories (see "Build a Town" and "Story Illustrations" below). If pictures are too lightweight to stick to the flannel board, cut strips of sandpaper and glue to the back of each, rough side out.

Build a Town

This is a continuing game. One day the convalescent might "build" a school building. He can go through magazines for pictures relating to school children, schoolrooms, play yards, books. Or he can draw his own pictures, which is more fun if he enjoys drawing. The pictures may be used to tell a story on a flannel board (above), or pinned to a curtain, or made into a simple scrapbook. Another day he might build a hospital, with nurses and doctors and medicines and flowers and new babies. Other suggestions: a home, a grocery store, a toy shop, a farm.

Story Illustrations

Pictures may be cut from a magazine, or drawn by hand, to tell a story read in a book. Paste to a large sheet of craft paper, or use on a flannel board (above).

MY OWN STORY: On a large sheet of paper, the convalescent can draw the foods eaten at the day's meals, or the people he has seen, or games and activities of the day. Or he can draw the story of his life (below).

Biography

The convalescent can make a scrapbook telling the life story of a character he has made up, or a storybook character, or the story of a real person. Or he can make a picture autobiography of his own life.

For these, pictures may be drawn or found in magazines, of babies doing different things, of a child going to school, older boys or girls biking or playing, grown people working. The pictures tell the story—of bad boy Joe and what made him change, or of Nancy who wanted to be a nurse, or whatever else the author wishes or the pictures suggest.

Miss Fancy's Come to Call (or Here Comes Clancy, for boys)

The convalescent pretends that a visitor has arrived and carries on a conversation with him. A parent can play this while working within easy hearing range. The parent or a brother or sister can be a neighbor, a favorite baseball player, the President of the United States, or anyone else desired.

Ways with Buttons

1. Sort them by color or size, putting different colors in separate small boxes.

2. Use buttons as food in doll games, spooning out with a soup spoon.

3. Make a button collection; ask friends to save pretty ones.

4. Make a mosaic for a decoration (p. 26).

5. String into a necklace by going through both holes of the button so that it lies flat. Lay buttons out in a line first to make a pleasing pattern.

6. Collect enough large buttons to sew to a band of elastic

for a belt. Or use grosgrain or felt, sewing small buttons on
in a pattern, such as a circle, triangle, or star.

Chart Your State

Draw the outline of your state on a large sheet of shelf or
wrapping paper. Send to the state tourist agency or a local
representative (p. 197) for travel literature, cut out pictures
from it and paste in the proper spots. Map the main cities,
rivers, highways and mountains (p. 200). Color lakes, harbors, mountains or deserts. Below important features print
statistics (size of city, height of mountain, etc.). Show products of special areas (one steer to represent cattle, an oil well,
orange tree, fish or field crop).

Calendars

WEATHER CALENDAR: Copy on craft paper the calendar of
the present month, or use a spare calendar. Each day place
a weather symbol to suit the day's weather: a sun, a cloud,
umbrella or drops of rain. At the end of the month count the
number of days for each, and list them. This gives an excellent picture of the local weather. For other weather observation, see p. 151.

PICTURE CALENDAR: On a large sheet (18 by 24 inches or
larger) of newsprint or wrapping paper make a calendar of
the present month. Use an almanac, the encyclopedia and
lists of your own family and church special days, birthdays,
etc., to find events for each date. Draw appropriate pictures
and label.

TOTEM-POLE CALENDAR: Use empty bathroom tissue rolls,
one for each month. Poster-paint each a different color or

combination, which can be symbolic of the month: red and
green for December, red, white and blue, or all red, for July,
etc.

For each month create a face or figure on the roll (Fig.
118). October, for example, could have two 6-inch orange
jack-o'-lanterns glued across front and back and glued together at the sides (A). The features could be carved through
both paper and tube, using a craft razor (p. 8).

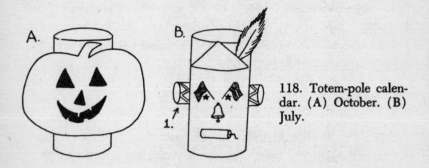

118. Totem-pole calen-
dar. (A) October. (B)
July.

July could have drums glued on for ears (B). On a strip of
paper draw the thongs (1) as shown. Tape the strip between
two milk-top disks. Cut two circles of white paper the size of
the milk tops and glue over them to cover the tape. Eyes
could be small flags from the five-and-ten or flags drawn from
craft paper. The nose might be a real little bell from the five-
and-ten, attached with pin or wire. For the mouth make a
firecracker of red craft paper rolled into a cylinder and held
with tape, a tiny piece of string dangling from the end. Make
a miniature soldier hat—a simple triangle with a band of red
or blue and a gay paper feather sticking from the top.

Hold totems together with tape, or glue one on top of the
other to an inside stick. Make four seasonal totems, with
three months in each.

Uses for Mail-Order Catalogues

1. Pictures for games, such as "Build a Town" (p. 187), "Story Illustrations" (p. 187), and "Biography" (p. 188).

2. Doll play pictures, paper dolls, stand-up pictures (p. 37).

3. Models to help draw your own pictures.

The Scribble Machine

Make a "scribble machine" by folding two or three sheets of white paper in half and stapling or tying together like a book (Fig. 119). On each page have family members—

119. Scribble machine.

even Baby—or friends scribble a mark. The convalescent adds to the scribble to make a figure, as shown by the dotted lines.

Almanac Play

1. If an almanac is available (inexpensive copies can be found in stationery stores), the convalescent can check daily to see what happened in history on that day.

2. Color paper napkins for the famiy dinner, using the day's events as the theme. Perhaps special craft items can be made for the occasion, such as Columbus' three ships on October 12.

3. Read up on the event in an encyclopedia or ask parents about the story of the event as they know it.

4. Act out the event in a puppet or counterpane theater (p. 193). If several events occurred, try to work all into the same skit.

5. Make a picture calendar (p. 189).

Helpful Fun

The convalescent often has a wonderful chance to help with family chores when the illness is not contagious. Here are several possibilities:

1. Restring all the broken strands of beads. Sort costume jewelry.

2. Help with the cooking. String beans, shell peas, crack nuts, break bread for stuffing, cut candied fruits for baking.

3. Have the family's drawers placed, one or two at a time, on a card table, and straighten them. Place small items in open boxes for greater neatness: socks, crayons and pencils, barrettes, ribbons.

Counterpane Travel

1. Pin up a world map and one of the United States. For this use a door, bulletin board, wallboard from a lumberyard (very inexpensive), or a string across the wall. The geographic areas can be looked up when mentioned in book or conversation: states, cities, rivers, countries, oceans.

2. Make a scrapbook of other countries or the United States (p. 127).

3. Write to local steamship, railroad, plane or travel agency offices for literature on special spots of interest. Plan make-believe trips there. Look up information in the encyclopedia.

4. Choose one country or state and draw a large map of

the area on shelf paper, wrapping paper or a market bag cut open. Cut out pictures of the area chosen and glue to the proper location. Thus for New York the choice might be the Statue of Liberty, for Washington, D.C., a picture of the White House, etc.

Counterpane Play

With a nurse's cap, a soldier hat or a cowboy sombrero, the convalescent can direct the activities of a hospital, a troop of men or a roundup. This can be completely imaginary, or small toys may be used.

For a counterpane train, see p. 87.

Counterpane Theater

Cut a side and the top from a medium-sized carton. Paste magazine pictures on the wall and floor for decoration and scenery: curtains, rugs, flowers, sometimes even a whole room scene from a magazine will suit. Or follow instructions for doll-house walls and furniture (p. 65), or use toy furniture.

Use miniature dolls, men, cars, etc., on this stage, and act out a story with them. Change voices for the different characters or use records for songs. Or the dolls can act out stories told on records.

Or give a complete puppet show. Make the puppets, the theater and scenery, as above; write several scripts so you can change to a new one from time to time.

Painting in Bed

Use poster paints or water colors, both washable. Place paints on a firm surface such as a card table. Cover the floor with oilcloth, plastic, rags or newspapers, and the bedclothes with plastic.

Whenever possible it is better, while in bed, to use paper and glue instead of paint, for covering drums for example.

Old Nosey

Draw a face in profile on cardboard, leaving it blank between eye and mouth, as in Fig. 120. Cut a small chain, such as a BB key chain, twice as long as the distance between eye

120. Old Nosey.

and mouth. Pierce holes in drawing at eye and mouth; force chain ends through holes and tape to the back of the cardboard. Shake the picture, causing the chain to form many different noses.

Clock

Mark a paper plate with the twelve numbers on the clock. Cut two arrows of different lengths from bright craft paper pasted on cardboard. Attach to the center of the plate with a brass paper fastener. The movable hands can be used to tell time.

The paper clock will also help pass the time. Set the hands at the time of the next visit from someone, or the time of the next pill, or at the hour that a brother or sister gets home from school, and watch for the real clock to match the toy.

References
Elizabeth Gets Well, Alfons Weber, M.D., Crowell, entertaining, reassuring. Almost any quiet indoor game or activity

mentioned in this book, including reading for pleasure, can serve as a convalescent activity. In addition, the following library references (descriptions of contents, pp. 3–4) are especially helpful: *Bibliography of Books for Children* (note, at back of book, special reference to convalescence, *Play: Children's Business*); also, for longer-term confinement or restriction, *The Best in Children's Books; Notes from a Different Drummer; The Bookfinder*, vol. 2.

READING FOR PLEASURE: BOOKS ARE FRIENDS

No childhood is complete without: Rudyard Kipling's two *Jungle Books* and *Just So Stories;* A. A. Milne's four *Winnie the Pooh Books;* and *Brer Rabbit Stories from Uncle Remus*, Joel Chandler Harris, Harper.

Other friends: *Christmas in the Woods*, Frances Frost, Harper; *A Wreath of Christmas Legends*, Phyllis McGinley, Macmillan. Grades 1–3: *The Tall Book of Bible Stories*, Katherine Gibson, Harper; *The Biggest, Smallest, Fastest & Tallest Things You've Ever Heard Of*, Robert Lopshire, Crowell; *The Day the Tide Went Out ... and Out ... and Out ...* , David McKee, Crowell; *Anno's Alphabet ... ; Anno's Counting Book*, Anno Mitsumasa, Harper, many awards. Grades 4–6: American Folklore Series: *Tomfoolery ... ; Whoppers* ... , etc., Alvin Schwartz, Lippincott; *The Golden Circle*, Hal Borland, Harper.

Poetry: *Sung Under the Silver Umbrella*, Dorothy Lathrop, Macmillan, a classic, ages 3–8. Grades 4–6: *Out of the Earth I Sing: Poetry and Songs of the Primitive Peoples of the World*, Grosset, primitive art; *Miracles: Poems by Children of the English-Speaking World*, Simon & Schuster (UNESCO); *Zero Makes Me Hungry*, compiled by Edward Lueders and Primus St. John, Lothrop, poems for today.

TRAVEL

At travel time activities are best that require no equipment at all, or very few easily handled and packed materials. Below are games, ideas and activities suited to the special needs of travel. Suggestions for camping and family excursions are also included.

WHAT TO TAKE

In addition to the sports equipment and clothes needed on arrival, keep wholesome snacks and thermos drinks on hand for the trip. Check the toy shelves carefully for easily handled games or activities that hold interest while taking little space.

Always pack a pad of paper, crayons, pencil, possibly even blunt scissors, glue or cellophane tape. A writing board from a five-and-ten or stationery store is inexpensive and will slip under the front seat for storage. A deck of cards and special travel-size games such as peg chess or peg checkers will be welcome if time is spent in trains, motels or hotels. A good book or two is always a good idea, and libraries usually permit longer lending in such cases. Add a song book and one of game suggestions such as those below. A soft ball, jump rope or other easily packed equipment for active play is often welcome when stopping for a while during the day.

Try to find room for any special hobby equipment that will make the trip more worth while, such as art materials, camera and film, or nature hobby supplies—materials to make plaster casts of woodland animals, for example (p. 170). Often a shoe box will hold all your needs.

Looking up on-the-spot references adds tremendously to the fun of travel, so take along nature identification booklets on rocks, trees, birds, flowers or other special interests. (To obtain, see the hobby that interests you under "Nature Lore.") Take also a shoulder bag to hold specimens.

WHAT TO BRING BACK

If possible, bring back interesting things you see. Private fields may not be entered of course, and nature items often should not be disturbed, but in spite of this traveling offers wonderful opportunities to add to collections. Sometimes there are stray plants of cotton on the edge of a field, or sprays of grain ready to harvest. Look for rock specimens, tarantula trap doors, cork or acorns from oak trees, for your collections. Keep an eye out for interesting pieces of dead-wood, seed pods or rushes for flower arrangements; moss, bark or cones for future crafts.

For a pressed flower collection, the rule on open lands where picking is permitted at all is to take a flower only where there are ten of the same variety within a square yard. Even then only one or two should be picked, and pressed immediately, because wild flowers wilt very quickly.

Other hobbies that profit from travel are coin collections, post-card or travel picture scrapbooks, history and geography.

WHAT TO SEE

Each state in the Union possesses an agency that will send travel literature. The materials they send will suggest many sights that unprepared travelers might overlook. The names of the agencies differ, but an envelope addressed to State Tourist Agency, and sent to the capital of the state you will pass through, should reach the proper destination. It is a good idea to list the area to be visited, and the approximate dates, so that information on special events may be included.

Look for these features while traveling:

1. First of all, don't miss national parks and monuments, which are spots of such unusual beauty or interest that they have been set aside for the American people to enjoy forever.

2. State parks, beaches, river or harbor tours, lakes, public gardens, zoos.

3. Place of historic interests in the section: Lincoln's log cabin, Sutter's Fort, the Liberty Bell. Read the leaflets that give the background.

4. Guided tours through industrial plants that are characteristic of the area: lumber mills, steel foundries, auto assembly lines.

5. Sections that retain an old or exotic atmosphere: the Cajun-French country west of New Orleans, the Pennsylvania Dutch region, San Francisco's Chinatown, and many others.

6. Check dates for special events, such as rodeos and logrolling contests in the Far West, folk festivals in Michigan or the Great Smokies.

7. Re-creations of the past: towns such as Dearborn, Michigan, Williamsburg, Virginia; homes from the Revolutionary era in New England; ante-bellum (pre-Civil War) homes of the South; museums with Indian or frontier displays.

8. Commercial playgrounds, such as Disneyland and various "fairylands."

GAMES TO PLAY IN THE CAR

Car-Counting Games

LICENSES: See who can spot the largest number of out-of-state licenses. One point may be given for each "foreign" license, indicating how many out-of-state cars there are on the road. Or one point may be given for each state, regardless of how many cars are seen from that state, indicating how many states are represented.

CAR-BUZZ, or CAR-FIZZ-BUZZ: Play these games (p. 201) by counting the cars you meet going in the opposite direction.

SUBTRACTION: Count the cars you meet, but subtract one for every car you pass or are passed by. For a very complicated game, play "Subtraction" and "Fizz-Buzz" (p. 201) at the same time.

LICENSE BINGO: Every time an out-of-state license is seen, the first to spot it says, "Bingo." Or, choose any number the players wish, such as number 4 and then every time a 4 is seen, call "Bingo." This can be combined with out-of-state cars. Thus Idaho AHJ424 would rate "Bingo, bingo, bingo," except in Idaho, where it would rate "Bingo, bingo."

Variation: A pencil record may be kept if desired. If this is done mark one column "out-of-state," one column by the number you are "collecting." Game is won by the first player to get ten in *each* column.

Observation Games

TRAVEL I SPY: One player is chosen to name something that all must watch for: a white horse or a red barn or a hitchhiker. The first one to see the object calls, "I spy," and then may choose the next object. If he chooses *white horse,* for example, and none is seen for some time, another player may call, "Time," and he must choose another object.

TRAVEL ABC: This is a type of "I Spy." Players look for letters of the alphabet in commercial signs, road markers, and

elsewhere. The letters must be found in order. Smaller children can look together for the letters; older children can com-
pete. If someone sees an "a" in "Apple Valley," he can claim
the first "a," but if his opponent is quick, he will see the "a"
in "Valley," too, and be able to claim one also.

ANIMAL FARM: Each player collects animals for his farm.
The first to see a tiger on a sign, for example, or a sheep in a
pasture, has that animal in his farm. At the end of a specified
time the one with the most animals wins.

Variation: Each player draws and corrals his animals on
paper as he sees them. Printed names may be added, as in a
zoo.

MAP GAMES:

1. Draw a map while traveling, marking in what is seen.
Have a sheet of paper for each hundred miles to be traveled.
For map symbols to use, see p. 172, or make up your own.
Make a key in the corner to identify the symbols.

2. Follow the road map while riding in the car, learning
what the symbols are, learning to read distances, looking for
special points of interest.

PIONEER: When crossing the desert, or other long stretches
of sameness, picture the family taking the trip by covered
wagon.

How far would it go in a day? What would you eat? What
would the wagon have in it? What water would you drink?
Is there a rise that would make a good campground? Could
it be defended from the Indians? Is there anything on the
"trail" that a pioneer would consider important, such as a
fork in the road, an arroyo to cross, a defile where an ambush
would be easy?

DESOLATION: When traveling through desolate country where little can be seen, or when traveling at night, decide upon sounds to represent certain objects that might be seen.

Thus a lizard in the road might be "Eek!" a tree in the desert, "Ah," a mileage sign, "Uh," another car, "Brrrr." Other sounds can be made up for any sights. When points of interest occur all at once, such as a car, a truck, a train, or a bridge, make all the sounds in a chain of sound.

Idea Games

THREE WORDS: Players take turns. Each chooses any three words he can think of and calls upon another player to make a sentence of them. Thus *mountains, box, rope,* may be used to say, "I carried a box lunch with a rope, and ate it when I reached the mountains."

BUZZ (nine years and up): Take turns counting, Player number 1 saying "One," next player, "Two," and on up. Every time a seven or a multiple of seven is used, say "Buzz" instead: 1-2-3-4-5-6-*buzz*-8-9 . . . 13-*buzz*-15 . . . The seventies would be *buzz*-1, *buzz*-2 . . . *buzz*-6, *buzz-buzz.*

BUZZ, JR. (six to eight years): Played as "Buzz," above, but "Buzz" is used in place of 10: 1-2-3-4-5-6-7-8-9-*buzz* . . .

FIZZ-BUZZ (nine years and up): Played as "Buzz," above, except that when 5 or a multiple is used, *fizz* is said instead: when 7 or a multiple is used, *buzz* is said. Those who miss drop out. Example: 1-2-3-4-*fizz*-6-*buzz*-8-9-*fizz*-11-12-13- *buzz* *fizz*-16.

FIZZ-BUZZ, JR. (six to eight years): The same as "Buzz, Jr.," except that 5 and 10 and their multiples are replaced: 1-2-3-4-*fizz*-6-7-8-9-*buzz*-11 . . .

DESCRIPTION: Players take turns describing any object they choose, using as many descriptive adjectives as they can think of: "The alligator is huge, horrid and hideous." "The brown-eyed Susan is pretty, fragrant and yellow." Younger players might say instead, "The brown-eyed Susan has a lot of petals and is like the sun," for the purpose of the game is to describe an object in as many ways as possible.

Variation: This can be played as a guessing game by saying, "I'm thinking of an animal that is huge, horrid and hideous." Other hints may be given as needed.

TWENTY QUESTIONS: Players take turns thinking of an object that is animal (live, or a product of a live animal, such as milk); vegetable (plant or product of a plant such as cotton); or mineral. Other players must guess in twenty questions or less. All answers must be "yes" or "no."

COFFEEPOT (six years and up): Played somewhat like "Twenty Questions," above, except that the word sought is always a verb—doing something. When others ask questions to discover what verb you are thinking of, all must use the word "coffeepot" as a substitute for the verb. Here is a simplified example of how the game is played: "Does everybody coffeepot?" "Yes." "Do they coffeepot at mealtimes?" "Yes." "Is it *eat*?" "No." "Drink milk?" "Yes."

TEAKETTLE (eight years and up): This is a game of *homonyms* (homo-nims), words that sound alike but mean something different. Substitute the word "teakettle" for the homonyms in a sentence, and the other players must guess the words in mind:

Example: "The *teakettle teakettled* the cowboy and was soothed." (. . . herd heard . . .). "The *teakettle* was one of a *teakettle* hanging from the tree; Mother will *teakettle* it."

(. . . pear . . . pair . . . pare. . .)

Here are several other homonyms: bear, bare; dear, deer; shoe, shoo; stair, stare; no, know; read, reed; here, hear; there, their; reel, real.

Variation: Each player may write a sentence containing *teakettle* words, and then read it aloud when time is called, for other players to guess.

THREE-FOURTHS OF A GHOST (ten years and up): One player begins by giving a letter of the alphabet. The next player adds a letter. It must not spell a finished word, but he must have a word in mind. Thus, if the first letter is *a* he might add *p*, thinking of *apple*. Each player adds a letter, being careful not to spell a word. If he spells a word, or can think of no letter to add on, he is one-fourth of a ghost. Thus the third player may add *t*, spelling *apt*, and become one-fourth of a ghost. If he instead adds *p* he is safe—for the moment. If he can think of no letter he or anyone else may challenge the previous player who, if he had no word in mind, is then one-fourth of a ghost. Each player is permitted three misses, until he is three-fourths of a ghost. On the fourth miss he is out. The winner is the last one in the game.

ASSOCIATION (six years and up): The one who is "It" says five words, and each player writes, or says aloud, the first word he thinks of when he hears each. If written, answers are read aloud later.

Variation: Players take turns calling a player's name, and then saying a word. The one called must instantly say what it makes him think of.

CATEGORIES (nine years and up): Choose some particular group of objects you wish to name. It can be a geographic group such as cities, mountains, rivers. It can be boys' or girls' names, animals, trees, flowers, or anything else desired.

Each player has a pencil and a large sheet of paper on which he writes the alphabet, leaving space for five or six names under or opposite each letter. Then, at a signal, the players attempt to write as many of the chosen group as they can think of under each letter. Give one point for each name, plus twenty-five points for a complete list—that is, at least one name under each letter. Call time when it is obvious that the players are running out of names or growing restive.

Variation (six years and up): The player who is "It" chooses a category, such as animals, or boys' names that begin with *B*, or any other choice. All players take turns adding to the list. Those who cannot add a word on three tries drop out. Or all players may make lists on paper and compare results when time is called. For younger players the game should be oral, or a written score may be kept by an adult.

IMAGINATION: This is a guessing game. "Where am I?" the one who is "It" asks. Other players begin to guess. The answers must be "yes" or "no," but if other players cannot locate "where," "It" may direct them with "warm" "hot," "red hot," "cold," "freezing," etc., since "It" may be in a place so small the others don't think of it at all—sitting on the horn, or behind the rear-view mirror, or in a trouser cuff.

AT THE MOTEL

Several games can be played in motels or their courts: sock toss (tossing a rolled pair of socks like a ball); balloon basketball, volley ball or baseball; cards; hide and go seek; dodge ball, various stunts. Few crafts lend themselves to travel, but these are possible: carving in soap (p. 13) or wood (p. 129)— both of these in the motel, not the car; making pipe-cleaner figures (p. 74); modeling in Plasticine (clay); weaving (p. 127); torn paper designs (p. 21); yarn flower (p. 28); wallet (p. 85).

Post-Card Puzzle

Buy a pretty post card to send to a friend, and on the back mark odd-shaped lines, making sections each very different from all others. Write a message, if desired, before cutting. Cut along the marked lines, making a puzzle. Mail in an envelope.

Freeze

To play this game, "It" says, "Freeze," when others least expect it, and all present must stop doing whatever they are doing *at that very moment*. People will be caught in all sorts of strange positions.

EXCURSIONS

In a file (p. 8) keep a list of interesting places to see. Of course the list will be headed with the nearest zoo, museum and playgrounds. When friends recount local trips, write them down for a future visit by the family.

The newspaper is another source of interesting excursions. It will list children's theaters, sports events, fairs, and special shows such as hobby, craft or Scout exhibits. It will report on what to see at particular times in public gardens or planetariums.

In addition to these, there may be an aquarium, a domestic animal farm, art centers, commercial fun spots such as "fairy-lands" or ocean piers nearby. You may live near an Indian museum, an Army installation, the home of a famous American, a university, a mission, fort or battleground. Some of the historic houses in your section may be open to the public. Jot these down, together with address and opening days or hours when possible.

Do not forget places of business that sometimes permit visitors or conduct tours: auto assembly plants, the post office, a newspaper office, the telephone and water-supply companies, a bakery. The warehouse and produce areas in the morning hours, canneries and nurseries, harbors and commercial fishing wharves, and many more industrial areas are fascinating spots to visit with the family.

Trip to a Junk Yard

One special excursion that can be full of surprises is a visit to a junk yard. Keep eyes and mind open, in order to find uses for novel items that may cost next to nothing. An old Navy stool may make an excellent doll table or outdoor seat. Large knocked-apart box sides might make fine walls for a lean-to against the garage, or old wheels fit for a home-made toy, or a great crate might serve as a doll house or fort.

CAMPING

Any vacation is fun, but many young people enjoy camping perhaps most of all. Often one year's vacation budget comes close to paying for the camping equipment that will serve for many years, and all items can be rented. If camping is not possible, try back-yard camping. (See *Backyard Games and Activities,* by Sylvia Cassell, Harper.)

Cooking Suggestions

Menu: Layered potato, baked apple or baked banana, milk or chocolate.

LAYERED POTATO: For each person take one baking potato, one cooking onion, one carrot, ¼ pound hamburger. Slice the unpeeled potato into three horizontal sections. Cut a one-foot square of heavy foil, or two one-foot squares of light foil. In this foil place the bottom layer of potato, a slice of onion, two slices of carrot side by side, a layer of half of the hamburger; then another layer of potato, onion, carrots, hamburger; and the top layer of potato. Wrap in foil and bake in coals one hour. This can be prepared at home, wrapped tightly at once and taken ready to bake.

BAKED APPLE: Cut out the core of the apple, being careful not to go through the bottom skin. Fill with sugar or brown sugar, wrap in foil, bake one-half hour in coals. If prepared ahead of time at home, seal the top of the hole with butter. Apples can be baked as they are, uncored, and will be even more wholesome.

BAKED BANANA: Cut a peeled banana almost through in one-inch slices. Into each slit insert a miniature marshmallow or slice of a marshmallow and one square of a small chocolate bar. Seal with foil. Bake in coals fifteen minutes.

Buddy Burner in Hobo Stove

In a tuna can tightly coil corrugated paper, standing the coils upright to the level of the can. Pour melted paraffin to

121. Buddy burner for camping.

fill the can, pouring over the coils, thus making a buddy burner (Fig. 121). When lighted, it will burn, producing a steady heat.

Place this in a #10 can turned upside down. The larger can must have holes cut with a canned-drink opener in the side near the bottom and another hole cut either in the top or on the side at the top. This is a hobo stove (Fig. 122).

The stove may be used without the buddy burner if a 3-by-3-inch hole is cut in the bottom of the #10 can, into which sticks can be fed, with a top or side top hole for the chimney. The dotted lines shown are for the hobo stove alone.

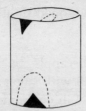

122. Hobo stove.

Ask at a restaurant for a #10 can, or substitute a 46-oz. grapefruit juice can.

Cooking suggestions for the stove: bacon, eggs, hot cakes, hot dogs, tomato half with cheese on top, canned beans or spaghetti.

Campfire Fun

Singing and storytelling are always campfire favorites. For a treat make "Samoas": toast two marshmallows; place these on a graham cracker, cover with four squares of a small chocolate bar, then cover this with another graham cracker. So good, everyone will want Samoa!

In the Woods

If you are interested in real camping, write to the National Campers and Hikers Association, 1507 National Newark Bldg., Newark 2, N.J., and ask for information concerning the organization.

References

The best way to learn to camp, and the most fun, is to join a youth group and use their manuals. There are many fine groups: the Boy Scouts and Girl Scouts, Campfire Girls, the YMCA and YWCA. Also: *The First Book of Camping*, by Edward C. Janes.

GENERAL TRAVEL REFERENCES

How to Travel with Grownups, Elizabeth Bridgman, Crowell, grades 1–3. All ages: *Visiting Our Past: American Historylands; Picture Atlas of Our Fifty States*; and *The New*

America's Wonderlands, National Geographic Society; *Washington (D.C.) for Children,* Ray Shaw, Scribner's. *Enchantment of Florida,* etc., stories of our states, a series, John Allen Carpenter, Children's Press.

THE UNITED STATES

All ages: *American Folk Songs for Children,* Ruth Crawford Seeger, Doubleday; and *The Story of Our National Ballads,* C. A. Browne and Willard A. Heaps, Crowell. Grades 5–8: *The American Flag,* Thomas Parrish, Simon & Schuster; *Flags of the USA,* David Eggenberger, Crowell; *State Flowers,* Anne O. T. Dowden, Crowell; *How We Named Our States,* Pauline Arnold and Percival White, Crowell; *The Young United States, 1783–1830,* Edwin Tunis, Crowell; *Ink, Ark and All That: How American Places Got Their Names,* Vernon Pizer; series: *An Album of . . . (. . . The Great Depression; . . . The Civil War,* etc.), Watts; *Stories of the States,* Frank J. Ross, Jr., Crowell; *A Book of Americans,* Rosemary and Stephen Vincent Benét, Holt; *This Land Is Mine,* Al Hine, ed., Lippincott, poems tracing our history.

UNDERSTANDING OUR WORLD

Manners Can Be Fun, and *Who Cares!,* Munro Leaf, Lippincott, grades 1–3. Grades 4–7: *Folk Tale Plays for Puppets: 13 Royalty-Free Plays for Hand Puppets, Rod Puppets or Marionettes,* Lewis Mahlmann, Plays Inc.; *Puppetry and Creative Dramatics in Storytelling,* Connie Champlin, Nancy Renfro Studio; *Costumes for You to Make,* Susan Purdy, Lippincott; *The Fireside Book of Fun & Game Songs,* Marie Winn, ed., Simon & Schuster; *Songs of the Chippewa,* John Bierhorst, Farrar, piano/guitar music; *Untune the Sky: Poems of Music & the Dance,* Helen Plotz, ed., Crowell; *Bridled with Rainbows: Poems About Many Things of Earth & Sky,* Sara and John E. Brewton, Macmillan.

Lost Civilizations, Leonard Cottrell, Watts; *Founding Mothers: Women in America in the Revolution Era,* Linda G. DePauw, Houghton; *As I Saw It: Women Who Lived the American Adventure,* Cheryl G. Hoople, Dial; *Women Who Win,* Francene Sabin, Random House, successful athletes; *The Farm Book,* Charles E. Roth and Joseph R. Froehlich, Harper.

ANIMALS TO ENJOY

Grades 1–3: *How Animals Behave,* Jeanne Bendick, *Parents* magazine; *Tooth and Claw: A Look at Animal Weapons* and *Getting Born,* Russell Freedman, Holiday House; *Red Tag Comes Back,* Fred Phleger, Harper; *Like Nothing at All,* Aileen Fisher, Crowell; *Animals in Winter,* Henrietta Bancroft and Richard G. Van Gelder, Crowell. Grades 4–6: *Misplaced Animals and Other Living Creatures,* Alice L. Hopf, McGraw-Hill; *Zoos of the World,* Robert Halm, Four Winds; *A Natural History of Marine Animals,* Victor Scheffer, Scribner's; *The Survivors: Enduring Animals of North America,* Jack Denton Scott, Harcourt; *Animals That Hide, Imitate and Bluff,* Lilo Hess, Scribner's; *View from the Oak,* Judith and Herbert Kohl, Scribner's; *Wild Animals I Have Known,* Ernest Thompson Seton, Doubleday.

Grades 1–3: *Metric Can Be Fun!,* Munro Leaf, Lippincott.

MATH AND ALL THAT

Grades 4–7: *The Code & Cipher Book,* Jane Sarnoff and Reynold Ruffins, Scribner's; *Exploring with Pocket Calculators,* Gary G. Bitter and Thomas H. Metos, Messner; *The I Hate Mathematics! Book,* Marilyn Burns, Little, Brown; *Imagination's Other Place: Poems of Science & Mathematics,* Helen Plotz, ed., Crowell; *The Creative Kid's Guide to Home Computers,* Fred D'Ignazio, Doubleday; *Magic House of Numbers,* Irving Adler, Crowell, puzzles, tricks.

INDEX

216

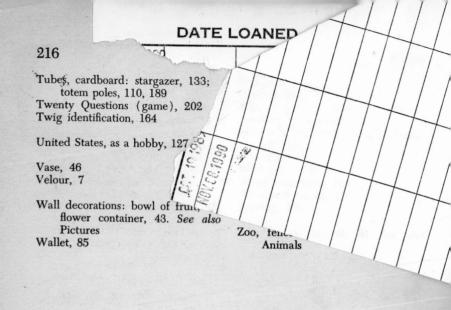